With Healing in His Wings

A Complete and Concise Presentation of God's Healing Gospel

by
Douglas H. Pessoni

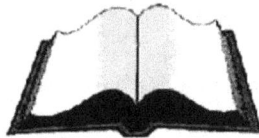

CCB Publishing
British Columbia, Canada

With Healing in His Wings: A Complete and Concise
Presentation of God's Healing Gospel

Copyright ©2008 by Douglas H.Pessoni
ISBN-13   978-0-9809191-9-6
Third Edition

Library and Archives Canada Cataloguing in Publication

Pessoni, Douglas H., 1941-
With Healing in His Wings: A complete and concise presentation of God's healing
gospel / written by Douglas H. Pessoni. – 3rd ed.
ISBN 978-0-9809191-9-6
1. Spiritual healing--Biblical teaching. 2. Healing--Religious aspects--
Christianity. 3. Faith--Biblical teaching. I. Title.
BT732.5.P48 2008   234'.131   C2008-902661-6

Cover design by Mark A. Pessoni

Publisher: CCB Publishing
             British Columbia, Canada
             www.ccbpublishing.com

Dedication

To God the Father for His immeasurable
love and His will to heal us;
to Jesus by whose redemptive act we
are both forgiven and healed;
and to the Holy Spirit by whose
power we are comforted and healed.

With Healing in His Wings

iv

Preface

The purpose of this book is to give people who are suffering from diseases and other medical conditions the faith necessary to be healed and made whole by the power of God. The book is a complete yet concise presentation of the biblical basis of divine healing. Since "...faith comes by hearing, and hearing by the word of God" (Rom. 10:17), this book will help build people's faith to a point where healing is appropriated.

The book is organized in a topical flow using comprehensive biblical references as support for the arguments being made. Therefore this book can serve not only to build an individual's faith but it can also serve as a reference text for pastors, teachers, evangelists, and for those in the healing ministry.

Faith healing is generally manifested in two ways: individual faith and intercessory faith. Individual faith healing relies on the person's own faith obtained by hearing and accepting the Word of God in regard to their own healing. Intercessory faith healing is when a person of faith prays for, lays hands on, anoints with oil, or uses other biblical methods for another individual. Both are equally valid and are synergistic when used in combination.

The fundamental principle underlying both is faith, faith in Jesus the Healer. Faith is both necessary and sufficient. Since there are often confusion and misunderstanding regarding faith, two chapters are devoted to this subject.

Faith healing is perhaps the least understood covenant blessing of God. It has been discredited and maligned by those from without and within the Body of Christ. Most of the objections raised over faith healing are based upon misconceptions and unfamiliarity about the underlying biblical truths. Therefore common misconceptions are addressed throughout the book and are refuted by scriptural truths. Each chapter ends with a summary of the scriptural truths. The summaries are collected in Chapter Twelve, The Tenets of Faith Healing.

I have chosen a modern Bible translation, the New King James Version, in order to add clarity and to avoid the drudgery of explaining archaic wording.

Words such as "disease," "sickness," or "condition," when used alone, are meant to include all physical and mental disease; maimed, deformed, dysfunctional, or disfigured bodies. Jesus can and does heal all of these conditions.

The author is deeply thankful to the following people for their help. Reverends Jim and Carolyn Hunter reviewed the doctrinal accuracy and gave me their encouragement. My sister, Day Ketcham, gave me valuable constructive criticism on the early manuscript adding to its readability. A friend, Kathleen Peterson, gave helpful suggestions on the nearly completed manuscript. I wish also to thank Alice Peppler of Alice 'n Ink for her professional and thorough editing and critiquing of the manuscript.

Most of all I thank the Holy Spirit, the true author and finisher of this book, for His inspiration, encouragement, insight, and strength.

May the healings which result from the reading of this book forever glorify God.

DHP
Hendersonville, Tennessee
March 2001

Contents

Preface v

Introduction 1

1. The Sources of Sickness and Healing 3

2. The Relationship between Medical Healing and Faith
   Healing 13

3. The Meaning and Importance of Faith 19

4. Growing One's Faith 31

5. The Will of God to Heal: Part I 36

6. The Will of God to Heal: Part II 44

7. Common Questions Concerning God's Will to Heal 50

8. The Timing of God's Healing 62

9. Proper Attitudes of the Heart and Mind 68

10. Appropriate Action 76

11. The Enemies of Faith and Healing 92

12. The Tenets of Faith Healing 101

    Epilogue 104

    Appendix I, Methods of Faith Healing 107

    Appendix II, Healing Testimonies 113

With Healing in His Wings

Introduction

*Now concerning spiritual gifts, brethren, I do
not want you to be ignorant:...gifts of healings
by the same Spirit.*

(1 Cor. 12:1, 9)

Faith healing can be defined as the healing of physical and
mental disease, the restoration of maimed, deformed,
dysfunctional, or disfigured bodies by the direct power of God
through faith. This faith is in the will of the Father to heal, the
redemptive healing act of Jesus, and the healing power of the
Holy Spirit.

The Bible clearly teaches that healing is available to all by
faith. Countless people, who have experienced first hand the
healing touch of God, often in miraculous ways, empirically
substantiate the validity of faith healing. Appendix II gives
examples of actual miraculous healings witnessed by the
author during the fifteen years in his healing ministry.

Faith healing is perhaps the least understood covenant
blessing of God. It has been discredited and maligned by those
from without and within the Body of Christ. Those in the
healing ministry are often considered as frauds and those being
healed are seen as either phonies or as having been
psychologically duped. These attitudes are frequently the
result of ignorance since many people have never heard the
true healing gospel.

Others find it difficult to believe that God, the Creator of
the universe, would ever interact personally with individual
human beings today. Still others make every effort to discredit

faith healing. If they allow themselves to believe that God is real and actively interacts with human beings, then they must face the reality of their own sinful nature. Many within the body of Christ reject it because they associate it with the Pentecostal or Charismatic Renewal movements which, for whatever reason, they consider peculiar. Again, these attitudes are not based on facts but rather ignorance or false conceptions. For those who are willing to believe, faith healing is a proven blessing of our loving God.

Christians put their faith in the redemptive blood of Jesus for their salvation. This faith comes by frequently hearing the word of God in this regard. It becomes second nature to them. The foundations of faith healing are presented in the Scriptures just as those of salvation. Since the healing gospel is less likely to be taught, it may seem foreign, yet its origins are the same, and it is equally valid.

Faith healing may be the only hope for those who have exhausted all medical means of healing without results. It can be relied upon for conditions and diseases for which there are no medical cures. It can also be an everyday ally in the battle against common illnesses and injury. Indeed, faith can lead to divine health as well as divine healing.

In reading this book people have a simple choice to make. They may decide to either believe it or not to believe it. If people are to appropriate their healing, they must believe the author of the Bible verses, the Holy Spirit. At the very least, they must read it with an open mind so that the Bible verses can speak to their hearts.

If some have never heard the healing Gospel before, they will be blessed by the truth that God wants them to be healed no matter how trivial or profound their condition may be.

Chapter One
The Sources of Sickness and Healing

The thief does not come except to steal, and to kill, and to destroy. I have come that they may have life, and that they may have it more abundantly.

(John 10:10)

Even when the physical causes of a disease or injury are known, philosophical and theological questions remain. "Why has this happened to me?" a person might ask. "How could a loving God let this happen to me or anyone else? If He created the earth, then He must have also created the cause of my condition." It is then natural for some people to blame God. Many people suffering under physical or mental disease find it difficult to believe that God will heal them if they see Him as the cause. If they are to believe in God—Father, Son, and Holy Spirit—for their healing, then it is important that they understand the truth of the matter.

The Scriptures show that when the Lord created the heavens and earth, He did not create disease or suffering.

Then God saw everything that He had made, and indeed it *was* very good (Gen. 1:31).

If everything, that is the universe, was *very good* then how could there have been anything as destructive and evil as disease? There is no mention of disease until after the fall of Adam and Eve in the Garden of Eden. Disease and suffering

3

came into the world through Satan in the same manner as sin. Therefore their cause, while physical in nature, is spiritual in origin.

> Put on the whole armor of God, that you may be able to stand against the wiles of the devil. For we do not wrestle against flesh and blood, but against principalities, against powers, against the rulers of the darkness of this age, against spiritual *hosts* of wickedness in the heavenly *places* (Eph. 6:11-12).

Here *the wiles of the devil* aptly describes disease among many other things.

> The thief does not come except to steal, and to kill, and to destroy. I have come that they may have life, and that they may have *it* more abundantly (John 10:10).

Disease steals people's vitality, productivity and joy; kills literally and figuratively; and destroys livelihoods, relationships, and dreams. Jesus has come to give people *abundant* life, a life free of disease.

The following passages show that Jesus overcame the disease wrought by Satan.

> When evening had come, they brought to Him many who were demon-possessed. And He cast out the spirits with a word, and healed all who were sick (Mat. 8:16),

> And behold, there was a woman who had a spirit of infirmity eighteen years, and was bent over and could in no way raise *herself* up. But when Jesus saw her, He

called *her* to *Him* and said to her, "Woman, you are loosed from your infirmity." And He laid *His* hands on her, and immediately she was made straight, and glorified God (Luke 13:11-13).

...how God anointed Jesus of Nazareth with the Holy Spirit and with power, who went about doing good and healing all who were oppressed by the devil, for God was with Him (Acts 10:38).

The ensuing passages plainly and directly state that Jesus is our healer.

For I *am* the Lord who heals you (Ex. 15:26).

And I will take sickness away from the midst of you (Ex. 23:25).

O Lord my God, I cried out to You,
And You have healed me (Ps. 30:2).

He sent His word and healed them,
And delivered *them* from their destructions (Ps. 107:20).

Heal me, 0 Lord, and I shall be healed (Jer. 17:14);

For I will restore health to you
And heal you of your wounds, says the Lord (Jer. 30:17),

The Sun of Righteousness shall arise
With healing in His wings (Mal. 4:2);

And Jesus said to him, "I will come and heal him" (Mat. 8:7).

For this purpose the Son of God was manifested, that He might destroy the works of the devil (1 John 3:8).

If Jesus came to destroy *the works of the devil* then He did not create those works. Therefore Satan is the source of all sickness, and Jesus is the source of all healing.

The Bible does mention times when the Lord brought diseases on the Egyptians (Ex. 15:26) and threatened the Israelites with disease (Deut. 28:21-22). To understand this, one must consider the differences between God's co-missive and permissive will. In the former case, the Lord would actively create the diseases and bring them upon people. This would be entirely inconsistent with a Savior who went about healing the sick. In the latter case, the Lord would simply permit diseases to strike people. It is quite obvious that the Lord permits disease, because if He did not, disease would not exist. It is in the same fashion that the Lord permits sin to exist in the world but does not create sin and bring it upon people.

James, in writing about the temptation to sin, states:

Let no one say when he is tempted, "I am tempted by God"; for God cannot be tempted by evil, nor does He Himself tempt anyone (James 1:13).

In the same way, let no one say when they are sick, "God made me sick," for God cannot be tempted by evil (disease), nor does He Himself make anyone sick. The assumption that God has made someone sick is totally contrary to the loving nature of God.

How can God be considered "loving" if He allows

(permits) sin and sickness to exist that cause such profound heartache and misery? Since the Bible in its entirety shows God to be loving, better one should ask, "Why does a loving God allow such heartache and misery?"

To understand this people must put themselves in God's place when He created human beings in His image. Humans would have to love God freely and be totally righteous to fellowship with Him. God could have created a robotic-type of human whom He could program to love Him in heart, word, and deed; however, this would definitely not be love at all because such humans would not love God by their own free will. Thus God had to create humans with free will.

However, free will is meaningless if there is no choice. So God had to allow the choice of obedience or disobedience. When humans disobey God's commands, they sin. Satan, who brought sin and disease into the world, provides the choice of sin. What is "sin" but a free will choice to turn away from God? What is "righteousness" but the rejection of Satan and the acceptance of Jesus Christ as Lord and Savior?

The only alternative God had for keeping people from such heartache and misery is not to have created them at all. This alternative was unthinkable in God's mind because He loves people so much.

> For God so loved the world that He gave His only begotten Son...(John 3:16),

This kind of love is very much like loving parents bringing children into the world knowing that they will suffer from sin and disease. The alternative is not to have children at all. What about young married couples who vow "to death do us part"? Do they consider the pain that they or their spouse would suffer if one were to die prematurely? No, because of

7

the love that they have for each other, the alternative of not marrying is unthinkable.

Through the atoning death and resurrection of Jesus, God gives people the opportunity to become righteous in spite of their sins. So also He gives people the opportunity to be healed in spite of their diseases. Both are free gifts dependent only upon faith in Jesus. Yes, the source of all sin and sickness is Satan, and the source of all forgiveness and healing is Jesus.

There are several commonly held misconceptions concerning the sources of sickness and healing:

Misconception:

"God is teaching me a lesson with this disease."

Yes, God can and sometimes does teach lessons with disease. However, the notion that Jesus sends down diseases to teach lessons is contrary to the many biblical teachings on God's love for mankind and His will and desire to see people healed. Would a sane, loving parent intentionally burn her young child on the stove to teach him that it is unsafe to go near the stove? If the child were to burn himself accidentally on the stove, this would be a lesson indeed. God does not send down diseases to teach people lessons, but He can teach them a lesson with the disease that Satan has placed on them. He can teach people to rely on Jesus to heal them of their diseases. He can also teach them humility and repentance.

It is no less absurd to assume that God sends down sickness to teach a lesson than to assume that He sends down sin for that purpose. Satan works both sin and sickness, not God.

Misconception:

"I am suffering this sickness for the glory of God."

Disease does not glorify God. Healing glorifies God.

So Jesus answered and said, "Were there not ten cleansed? But where *are* the nine? Were there not any found who returned to give glory to God except this foreigner" (Luke 17:17—18)?

Jesus had just healed the ten lepers and only one came back to give Him thanks and praise, that is *to give glory to* God for healing him.

Most are familiar with the account of Jesus raising Lazarus from the dead.

Therefore the sisters sent to Him, saying, "Lord behold, he whom You love is sick." When Jesus heard *that,* He said, "This sickness is not unto death, but for the glory of God, that the Son of God may be glorified through it" (John 11:3-4).

Clearly, He was not glorified by the disease but by the resurrection (healing) of Lazarus. Jesus said:

By this My Father is glorified, that you bear much fruit; so you will be my disciples (John 15:8).

How effectively can people *bear much fruit* for the Lord when they are sick? Sickness brings glory to Satan. A person's healing through faith glorifies God.

The sickness and suffering of the Father's children sadden Him just as sick children sadden loving parents. Jesus is also saddened because He has suffered so much for people's healing:

> But He *was* wounded for our transgressions,
> *He was* bruised for our iniquities;
> The chastisement for our peace *was* upon Him,
> And by His stripes we are healed (Is. 53:5).

Misconception:

"God is punishing me because of what I did."

There are two possible reasons for this line of thinking. First, a person may have contracted a disease through some sinful activity. Second the sinful activity could not have caused the disease, yet the person links the disease with his activity. In both cases he sees God as vengeful and may point to Deuteronomy where the Lord tells the Israelites:

> But it shall come to pass, if you do not obey the voice of the Lord your God, to observe carefully all His commandments and His statutes which I command you today, that all these curses will come upon you and over take you (Deu. 28:15):

These curses are known as "The Curse of the Law" and include virtually every disease known to mankind. However:

> Christ has redeemed us from the curse of the law, having become a curse for us (for it is written, *"Cursed is everyone who hangs on a tree")* (Gal. 3:13),

Since the Lord has redeemed us from diseases, He can not punish His people (believers) with them. This does not mean that they will not suffer the natural consequences of certain sinful activities, however. God has already forgiven people of their sins and healed them of their diseases. One needs only to take what is actually theirs through repentance and faith.

Bless the Lord, O my soul,
And forget not all His benefits:
Who forgives all your iniquities,
Who heals all your diseases (Ps. 103:2-3),

who Himself bore our sins in His own body on the tree, that we, having died to sins, might live for righteousness—by whose stripes you were healed (1 Peter 2:24).

Misconception:

"God used disease to bring that person home to heaven."

The implication here is that God wrought disease on the person that caused his death. God's will is for all believers to live a long, prosperous life.

My son, do not forget my law,
But let your heart keep my commands;
For length of days and long life

And peace they will add to you (Pr. 3:1-2).

With long life I will satisfy him,
And show him My salvation (Ps. 91:16).

Even if the person had a long, prosperous life, God would not use the wiles of the Devil to bring His servant home. But, be assured that God will welcome his "good and faithful servant" (Matt. 25:23) home no matter if he died of a disease or not.

Some will ask, "How can a person die if he does not get sick?" The answer is that the body will eventually wear out and stop functioning. Arguments that, if the body stops functioning then the cause of the death is still a disease, are incorrect since God allows the body to wear out with age. This would be a death of "natural causes."

Summary

The Scriptures plainly teach that Jesus is the source of all healing and that Satan is the source of all disease. God does not bring disease upon His people but permits disease to exist in the same manner and for the same reason that He permits sin to exist. This permission shows His love for mankind.

Since God is the source of all healing, then what do the Scriptures say about the relationship of medical healing to faith healing? This is discussed in the next chapter.

Chapter Two
The Relationship between
Medical Healing and Faith Healing

Luke the beloved physician and Demas greet you.
(Col. 4:14)

What is the relationship between medical healing and faith healing? This question has been debated for decades if not for centuries. The debate covers two extremes in thinking.

At one extreme are those who have little or no faith in divine healing but hold great faith in medical healing. They frequently believe that given enough time medical science will come up with cures for virtually all diseases and medical conditions. If they contract a disease for which there is no traditional cure, then they will frequently seek non-traditional medical cures.

The other extreme has such great faith in Jesus the Healer that they hold medical healing in disdain. When someone who has been under medical care for years without results is miraculously cured by faith in Jesus, they will jeer at the doctors' efforts. They may fear that going to a medical practitioner would violate their faith. This group is quick to point out the shortcomings in medical practice. They also point out, and rightfully so, that when medical cures are ineffective or nonexistent, faith in Jesus the Healer is their only hope.

The fallacy in both of these positions is that they fail to see that Jesus is the source of *all* healing, both divine and medical.

The Scriptures have much to say about this matter.

Now a certain woman had a flow of blood for twelve years, and had suffered many things from many physicians. She had spent all that she had and was no better, but rather grew worse. When she heard about Jesus, she came behind *Him* in the crowd and touched His garment; for she said, "If only I may touch His clothes, I shall be made well" (Mark 5:25-28).

Jesus miraculously healed this woman. By itself this Scripture seems to support the faith healing side; however, in the context of other passages, this primarily shows that the Scriptures recognize the realistic limitations of medical healing.

And in the thirty-ninth year of his reign, Asa became diseased in his feet, and his malady was *very* severe; yet in his disease did not seek the Lord, but the physicians. So Asa rested with his fathers; he died in the forty-first year of his reign (2 Chron. 16:12-13).

This Scripture too would seem to support the faith healing side of the argument, but notice that the physicians were not condemned, rather Asa simply didn't seek the Lord for his healing. It also implies that if he had, he likely would have been healed.

Other Scriptures tend to support the medical side.

A merry heart does good, *like* medicine (Pr. 17:22),

Here the Scriptures recognize that medicine does good. Jesus, Himself, also implied that medical healing was effective.

"Those who are well have no need of a physician, but those who are sick. I did not come to call *the* righteous, but sinners, to repentance" (Mark 2:17).

Jesus is countering those who criticized Him for associating with sinners. This would not be an effective analogy if physicians did not heal the sick. So the Scriptures also recognize the effectiveness as well as the limitations of medical healing. God worked "unusual miracles" of healing through the hands of Paul (Acts 19:11-12). However, in his letter to the Colossians, Paul clearly expresses reverence for the medical healing profession.

Luke the beloved physician and Demas greet you (Col. 4:14).

By calling Luke *the beloved physician*, it is clear that Luke continued in the role of a physician during his apostolic ministry. Peter is never referred to as "the beloved fisherman" or Matthew as "the beloved tax collector." Therefore this shows esteem for the profession of physician as well as for Luke himself.

Paul advised Timothy to:

No longer drink only water, but use a little wine for your stomach's sake and your frequent infirmities (1 Tim 5:23).

This clearly shows the use of medicine among the believers. It is no wonder that Christian religious orders have founded so many medical hospitals, not to mention those people of God who enter into the medical missionary field.

15

It must be said, however, that there are no medical healings that have not also been appropriated solely through faith in Jesus the Healer. Also, there are multitudes of faith healings of conditions for which there are no medical cures. So then, the Scriptures recognize both the effectiveness and limitations of medical healing and hold it in high esteem. This is no wonder since Jesus is the source of all healing, both divine and medical. Furthermore, as we saw in the case of Asa, the Scriptures criticize those who seek medical healing without also seeking God. Therefore we can conclude that faith healing and medical healing are allies created by God to thwart sickness. They are not contrary to one another. Moreover we know from prolific physical evidence that the two healing methods are synergistic; that is, they each tend to increase the effectiveness of the other when used together.

There are several misconceptions concerning the relationship between medical healing and faith healing:

Misconception:

"He was healed by the medicine not by Jesus."

"He was healed naturally by his immune system not by spiritual means."

The problem here is that healing is segregated into the two camps previously mentioned. It is the kind of dualistic thinking that says it is either one or the other but not both that caused the healing. They fail to see that Jesus is behind both types of healing—Jesus is the source of *all* healing. People should praise Him when they are healed by their medicine. They should praise Him for giving man the knowledge and skill to bring about their healing.

This dualistic kind of thinking can be manifested when a person who has been relying strictly on spiritual healing relents, takes medicine, and is then healed. It is natural for someone like this to think and say that the medicine and not faith in Jesus is what healed him.

This is very much like the man who was working on the steep roof of a very high building. He lost his footing and started sliding faster and faster toward the edge of the roof and certain doom. In his desperation, he called out, "Lord, save me!" Just then his pants caught on a large nail, and he stopped cold inches from the edge. In his relief he said, "Never mind, Lord, my pants caught on a nail." Now we may laugh at this man's blindness, but it is not much different when it comes to healing.

Misconception:

"He was healed by Jesus not by the medicine."

Bias exists on the faith side as well. This statement would be true if it were to imply that Jesus was responsible for the medicine's effectiveness; however, this bias frequently shows disdain for medicine rather than seeing it as an ally to faith healing.

Misconception:

"It is a violation of faith in Jesus the Healer to use medical healing."

This statement may or may not be true, depending on the person's understanding and attitude toward both medical and faith healing.

If faith for healing were abandoned for medical healing, then it certainly would be a violation of faith. However, if the hand of God is seen in medical healing and Jesus is seen as the source of *all* healing, then medical healing can be a synergistic ally to faith healing. The Scriptures themselves give witness to this fact.

It is very important for people under medical supervision to stay under that supervision until their medical doctor pronounces them healed. It is not an appropriate act of faith to throw out one's medicine as God may be working His healing through that medicine. Even if some are miraculously and instantaneously healed through faith, they should not stop taking their medicine until their doctor says it is all right to do so.

A lady who had severe rheumatoid arthritis struggled with the question of whether seeking medical healing was a violation of her faith or not. She went to a doctor who prescribed appropriate medication. A friend advised her to say, "In the name of Jesus!" each time she took a pill. This simple act of faith, among many others, brought about her eventual total healing of this crippling disease.

Summary

The Scriptures recognize both the limitations and effectiveness of medical healing and hold it in high esteem. This is consistent with the teaching that Jesus is the source of *all* healing, both divine and medical. The Scriptures criticizes those who seek medical healing without also seeking God. Faith healing and medical healing are allies against sickness, not contrary to one another. They each increase the effectiveness of the other when used together.

The next chapter discusses faith—what it is and why it is so necessary for appropriating one's healing.

Chapter Three
The Meaning and Importance of Faith

Now faith is the substance of things hoped for,
the evidence of things not seen.

(Heb. 11:1)

The importance of faith in Jesus cannot be overstated. Mankind's very salvation depends upon it (Acts 26:18, Rom. 3:28, Eph. 2:8). Furthermore, the author of Hebrews states:

But without faith *it is* impossible to please *Him* (Heb. 11.6),

It is also clear from the Scriptures that faith in Jesus brings about one's healing.

And the prayer of faith will save the sick, and the Lord will raise him up (James 5:15).

for she said to herself, "If only I may touch His garment, I shall be made well." But Jesus turned around, and when He saw her He said, "Be of good cheer, daughter; your faith has made you well." And the woman was made well from that hour (Mat. 9:21-22).

Then He touched their eyes, saying, "According to your faith let it be to you." And their eyes were opened (Mat. 9:29—30).

And His name, through faith in His name, has made this man strong, whom you see and know. Yes, the faith which *comes* through Him has given him this perfect soundness in the presence of you all (Acts 3:16).

From these passages it is easy to see where the term "faith healing" comes from. It is one's faith in Jesus the Healer that brings forth his or her healing.

Chapter One showed that Satan is the source of all sickness. Faith also gives believers power and authority over him.

And this is the victory that has overcome the world— our faith (1 John 5:4).

Here *the world* refers to Satan and his domain. Through faith believers have victory over Satan and his works—sin and sickness.

above all, taking the shield of faith with which you will be able to quench all the fiery darts of the wicked one (Eph. 6:16).

Fiery darts aptly describes disease among other things, and quenching a disease means to be healed from it.

It is therefore very important to understand what faith is and what it is not. While there is much confusion over the meaning of faith, the Scriptures define faith in the following manner:

Now faith is the substance of things hoped for, the evidence of things not seen (Heb. 11:1).

Webster's New Collegiate Dictionary defines "substance" as the "ultimate reality that underlies all outward manifestations and change." So faith is the "ultimate reality" of the things people are hoping for, the manifestation of their healing. Notice that faith is not hope, although hope plays an important part in faith. Many people hope for their healing or restoration. Faith, however, is the reality of their healing. The same dictionary defines "evidence" as something that furnishes proof. Therefore faith itself furnishes the proof of the ultimate reality of their healing in spite of the fact that they are racked with the symptoms of disease. As someone once pointed out, facts change, truth does not. Faith in the truth of God's Word brings about the manifestation of healing, a change in the facts.

The biblical definition of faith includes the phrase "of things not seen." Therefore faith does not depend on what is seen, felt, or experienced, including the symptoms of the disease. This type of evidence has no place in faith. Faith in the Word of God is the evidence. The Scriptures repeat this point several times.

For we walk by faith, not by sight (2 Cor. 5:7).

Then Jesus said to him, "Unless you *people* see signs and wonders, you will by no means believe" (John 4:48).

Jesus said to him, "Thomas, because you have seen Me, you have believed. Blessed *are* those who have not seen and *yet* have believed" (John 20:29).

People's symptoms testify that they are sick; the Word of God says they are healed. Faith says they believe the truthfulness of Word of God and not the reality of their symptoms. Oh yes, the symptoms are there screaming at them that they are not healed, but since they "walk by faith" these symptoms become irrelevant.

It is instructive to look at some other examples of biblical faith in action.

Simon (later named Peter) was a career fisherman. He knew when the fish were there and when they were not.

Now when He had stopped speaking, He said to Simon, "Launch out into the deep and let down your nets for a catch." But Simon answered and said to Him, "Master, we have toiled all night and caught nothing; nevertheless at Your word I will let down the net." And when they had done this, they caught a great number of fish, and their net was breaking (Luke 5:4—6).

Simon's life long experience as a fisherman told him that there were no fish to be caught. Nevertheless Simon believed Jesus' word to such a point that he took action in spite of what he knew was the reality of the situation. Jesus, the Creator of the universe, can and does change reality.

Abram was a man of God who was very wealthy but had no children through his wife Sarai because she could not conceive. Although they were both very old, the Lord promised Abram that he would become "a father of many nations" and renamed him Abraham (Gen. 17:4-5).

And not being weak in faith, he did not consider his own body, already dead (since he was about a hundred years old), and the deadness of Sarah's womb (Rom. 4:19).

Notice that the reality of Abram's world was that he and his wife Sarai (later named Sarah) were childless and extremely old and that Sarai was well beyond menopause. However, they ignored these facts and took appropriate action. The birth of Isaac was not a virgin birth. Abram and Sarai needed to conceive the child naturally, and based on their faith they did just that. Without faith this would have seemed naive and foolish.

By faith Noah, being divinely warned of things not yet seen, moved with godly fear, prepared an ark for the saving of his household, by which he condemned the world and became heir of the righteousness which is according to faith (Heb. 11:7).

It must have seemed ridiculous to those not sharing Noah's faith to see him labor for years building a huge vessel on dry land. Even for Noah it must have been difficult to visualize the enormity of the flood before it actually happened. Yet in spite of what he did not see, he took the action of building the ark.

So then faith has several components that need to be satisfied. First is an understanding of what God has said and promised in His word. Next is an absolute belief in God's promise to a point where it becomes a reality in one's heart and mind. Third is the discounting of any physical evidence that contradicts God's Word. And fourth is appropriate action based on that belief.

To summarize, Biblical faith is the absolute belief in a promise revealed by God, in spite of no evidence or contrary evidence, to a point where it becomes reality in one's heart and mind and appropriate action is taken.

When someone has faith for his or her healing it becomes self-evident.

And behold, they brought to Him a paralytic lying on a bed. And Jesus, seeing their faith, said to the paralytic, "Son, be of good cheer; your sins are forgiven you" (Mat. 9:2).

This man heard Paul speaking. Paul, observing him intently and seeing that he had faith to be healed, said with a loud voice, "Stand up straight on your feet!" And he leaped and walked (Acts 14:9-10).

Just what did Jesus and Paul see that convinced them that these people had the faith to be healed? Why joy and peace, the fruit of the Spirit (Gal. 5:22), in spite of these men being racked with the symptoms of their diseases.

Now may the God of hope fill you with all joy and peace in believing, that you may abound in hope by the power of the Holy Spirit (Rom. 15:13).

One does not have to be in the healing ministry very long before he or she can tell which people have the faith to be healed. Peace and joy are reflected in their eyes and face. People can not feign peace and joy. Peace and joy come from a faith that they know that they are about to be healed. Their healing has become a reality before it is manifested. There is no fear and doubt. When peace and joy are not present then faith for healing is not present. This is not being judgmental but rather simply stating the facts.

Specifically for healing, faith is characterized by the following components. First is an understanding of what God has said and promised in His word, that it is absolutely His will to heal anyone who asks Him in faith. This will be proven later in Chapters Five and Six. Next is the absolute belief in

God's promise to a point where healing becomes a reality in one's heart and mind. Third is the discounting of disease's symptoms. As shown in Chapter Five, the symptoms contradict God's Word that says that Jesus has already done what is necessary for the healing. And fourth is appropriate action based on that belief. Chapter Ten is devoted to showing what is appropriate action for one's healing.

Some things masquerade as faith and are frequently confused with faith.

Hope is an important component of faith, and it is impossible to have faith without hope. But hope is not faith. In discussing believers' redemption through the blood of Christ, Peter states:

who through Him believe in God,
who raised Him from the dead and gave Him glory, so
that your faith and hope are in God (1 Peter 1:21).

Notice that a distinction is made between faith and hope. Hope gives people the motivation to seek the truth about faith healing in the Scriptures. Hope also gives one the motivation to read this book. While hope does give people a certain expectation for healing, it does not give them the absolute assurance that they will be healed.

Belief is another essential component of faith, but in itself it is not faith. Belief is typically arrived at through an examination of a body of evidence; however, faith requires belief without that body of evidence and perhaps even in the face of contrary evidence. Belief must be based on the Word of God only. Often when God heals people and the symptoms return, they immediately start basing their belief on the results of the previous healing. This is belief based on physical facts

25

not on the Word of God. If their symptoms come back they should go back to the Word of God, the Bible.

Mental assent is an intellectual agreement with the Word of God but not an absolute belief that makes healing a reality in people's hearts and minds. Mental assent rarely causes people to take appropriate action, and it never results in the peace and joy that faith brings. People cannot simply agree with the Word of God. It has to get into their hearts.

> that if you confess with your mouth the Lord Jesus and believe in your heart that God has raised Him from the dead, you will be saved (Rom. 10:9).

This does not say, "believe in your mind" or simply "believe." People are dealing with spiritual things here, not intellectual things. People's "hearts" are their inner beings, their spirits. They do not need to be smart or have intellectual prowess to be healed. They need only to trust the Word of God in a child-like fashion (Mark 10:15). This may offend some people's intellectual upbringing, but they should not reject the Word of God.

Presumption manifests itself in many ways disguised as faith. Presumption takes liberties with God's healing Gospel. It says that if it is God's will to heal people than they don't have to be concerned with health matters. Presumption keeps one away from medical healing when it is clearly called for (see Chapter Two). Healing, just as salvation, is a gift of the sovereign God. It cannot be presumed upon. It can only be appropriated through faith.

There are several misconceptions concerning the meaning and importance of faith:

Misconception:

"I hope God will heal this."

This statement is a sure sign that the person has not reached a point in his or her heart which can be called faith. This type of healing is not called "hope healing," it is called *"faith healing."* Faith says, "I am healed! Thank you, Jesus!" One must move on from hope and build faith.

Misconceptions:

"I guess I'm not healed because I still have the symptoms."

"Well I guess I really wasn't healed because my symptoms are back."

"I've had hands laid on me several times, and I'm still not healed.

These declarations are statements of fact. If people still have symptoms then they are still sick. However, if they have faith, then the reality in their heart is that they are already healed. Statements such as these, while based on physical evidence, are a sure way to undermine people's faith. Remember that the Scriptures say to walk by faith not by sight. These kinds of statements should be kept out of their vocabulary. The statements show faith in Satan, not in Jesus.

Misconceptions:

"I'll believe it when I see it."

"God, show me a sign that You are willing to heal me."

"If God heals this, then I'll really believe in faith healing."

These statements are putting the cart before the horse. Faith demands that people believe it *before* they see it. Faith says, "I don't need any signs. God's Word says it, and that settles it." Remember what Jesus Himself said:

Then Jesus said to him, "Unless you *people* see signs and wonders, you will by no means believe" (John 4:48).

Jesus said to him, "Thomas, because you have seen Me, you have believed. Blessed *are* those who have not seen and *yet* have believed (John 20:29).

Misconceptions:

"I'll try faith healing and see what happens."

"Since I've got nothing to lose, I'll try faith healing."

Trying faith healing is pointless. Trying says people really don't believe in faith healing, and it is therefore not faith. Unless they are willing to totally immerse themselves in the Word of God and make a concerted effort to build their faith, they are wasting their time. Chapter Four shows how to build faith.

Misconceptions:

"That person has more faith than anyone else I know, but he is still sick.'

"I knew someone who had faith in God to heal them and he died from the disease."

These types of statements typically show a misunderstanding of what faith is. Generally, the sick person being spoken of may not have faith at all, but one or more of the impostors discussed earlier.

Another possibility is that the person being spoken of has a strong faith for his or her salvation but not for healing. It is common to confuse the two. Also the person may have reached a point in their illness where they have accepted their perceived ultimate fate of dying. Elizabeth Kubler-Ross, in her landmark book, *On Death and Dying,* called this emotional experience "acceptance." Acceptance is usually the last emotional experience before death. At this point the person may not want to be healed and continue to face the struggles and hardships in this life. At one time Jesus asked a man at the Pool of Bethesda if he wanted to be healed.

Now a certain man was there who had an infirmity thirty-eight years. When Jesus saw him lying there and knew that he already had been *in that condition* a long time, He said to him, "Do you want to be made well?" (John 5:5-6)

Now this question might seem absurd, but some people do not want to be healed for any number of reasons. They may have reached the point of acceptance, or perhaps their condition has given them the attention or sympathy that they crave in their lives.

It is also very difficult for people to build their faith for healing when people with no faith surround them. Pity, fear, and distress may seem compassionate but they undermine faith.

Summary

Biblical faith is the absolute belief in a promise revealed by God, in spite of no evidence or contrary evidence to a point where it becomes reality in one's heart and mind and appropriate action is taken. The importance of faith in Jesus cannot be overstated. People's salvation and healing depend upon it, and without it they can not please God.

The next chapter discusses how to build one's faith.

Chapter Four
Growing One's Faith

So then faith comes by hearing, and hearing by the word of God.

(*Rom. 10:17*)

The last chapter discussed the importance of faith in appropriating one's healing. This chapter shows how to grow that faith.

God has dealt to each one a measure of faith (Rom. 12:3).

From this Scripture it is evident that all people have some measure of faith in their spiritual lives. Because this may not be the level of faith that appropriates healing, people must build upon the faith they already have.

Now this is the confidence that we have in Him, that if we ask anything according to His will, He hears us. And if we know that He hears us, whatever we ask, we know that we have the petitions that we have asked of Him. (1 John 5:14-15).

What wonderful news this is! If people know that it is His will to heal them, then they can ask for healing and it will be manifested. However, people cannot have sustaining faith for their healing until they know that it is God's will to heal them. How are they to know His will in this matter? It is by reading and searching God's Word to see that it is His will to heal them.

These are more fair-minded than those in Thessalonica, in that they received the word with all readiness, and searched the Scriptures daily to *find out* whether these things were so (Acts 17:11).

Paul brings this point home more clearly.

So then faith *comes* by hearing, and hearing by the word of God (Rom. 10:17).

Note the passage does not say that faith comes by *having heard* the Word of God. It says that people are to keep on reading that Word. They should search the Scriptures daily to see if these things be so. This will not only increase their faith for healing but will be a blessing in many other ways.

When Paul wrote this, Jesus had already died, been resurrected, and had ascended into Heaven. So how could the Romans to whom Paul was writing, or the people of today for that matter, *hear* the "word of God"? Fortunately, God has left His Word for mankind in the Bible. Some may say, "It is one thing to hear God speak and quite another to read it in the Bible." That is not so. It is instructive to look at someone who heard Jesus speak directly to him and see how the Bible reports it.

The nobleman said to Him, "Sir, come down before my child dies!" Jesus said to him, "Go your way; your son lives." So the man believed the word that Jesus spoke to him, and went his way. And as he was now going down, his servants met him and told *him,* saying, "Your son lives" (John 4:49-51)!

Notice that the man believed *the word* that Jesus spoke to him. It does not say that the man "believed Jesus," but that he believed His word. Naturally, the man did believe Jesus because believing His word is the same as believing Him. Some will say, "If only I had been there with Jesus. If I had heard Him speak healing directly to me, I certainly would have believed that it was His will." But in the parable of the rich man and the beggar Lazarus, Jesus points out:

"But he said to him, 'If they do not hear Moses and the prophets *(i.e. the written word),* neither will they be persuaded though one rise from the dead'" (Luke 16:31).

Many people heard Jesus speak directly to them but didn't believe Him. The nobleman whose child was healed heard Jesus speaking directly to him. He not only believed Jesus but he also believed His word. The Bible is God's Word to each individual personally. It speaks of one's personal redemption and personal healing. Therefore the people who heard Jesus speak healing directly to them had no advantage whatsoever over people today who have God's written word, the Bible.

The Scriptures show that the "Word of God" is synonymous with Jesus Himself.

He sent His word and healed them,
And delivered *them* from their destructions (Ps. 107:20).

In the beginning was the Word, and the Word was with God, and the Word was God...And the Word became flesh and dwelt among us, and we beheld His glory, the

33

glory as of the only begotten of the Father, full of grace
and truth (John 1:1, 14).

Then I saw heaven opened, and behold, a white horse.
And He who sat on him *was* called Faithful and True,
and in righteousness He judges and makes war...and
His name is called The Word of God (Rev. 19:11, 13).

The Scriptures say clearly and directly that healing is
appropriated through the reading of the Bible.

My son, give attention to my words;
Incline your ear to my sayings.
Do not let them depart from your eyes;
Keep them in the midst of your heart;
For they *are* life to those who find them,
And health to all their flesh (Pr. 4:20-22).

This passage speaks also about the continuous nature of
one's Bible reading. It seems that building one's faith is like
filling a vessel with a hole in the bottom with water. If the
water represents the Word of God, then the level of water in
the vessel represents the level of one's faith. The more water
one adds, the higher the level rises. Stop adding water or slow
down the rate of addition and the level will start to drop. The
vessel may even run dry. Abandoning the Word of God
inevitably results in lost faith.

The next two chapters reveal the wealth of Scriptures that
show clearly that is it God's will to heal anyone who comes to
Him in faith.

There is one major misconception concerning the growth of
one's faith through Bible reading.

Misconception:

"The Bible is full of contradictions and mistakes. It can't be trusted literally."

It is not the intent of this book to enter into a debate on biblical accuracy. Modern "higher criticism" has lead many to distrust the Bible, thus leading some to abandon the faith altogether. It is not necessary to believe in the uncanny accuracy of the Bible through faith alone. Abundant evidence, based on history, archeology, and fulfilled historical prophecy stand as testimonies to the Bible's remarkable accuracy.

Almighty God, who sent His only begotten Son to die for people's sins, would not entrust His promise of love and forgiveness, people's very salvation, to a document full of errors. People's faith will be seriously compromised if they do not believe the truth of the Bible.

Summary

Continual reading and believing God's Word, the Bible, increases faith for people's healing. By doing this they will learn that it is God's will to heal them.

The next two chapters prove from the Scriptures that it is absolutely God's will to heal everyone who comes to Him in faith.

Chapter Five
The Will of God to Heal: Part I

...And by His stripes we are healed.

(Is. 53:5)

This chapter shows how physical healing is an integral part of God's redemption plan for mankind and the redemptive act of Jesus on Calvary. If people believe that Jesus died for their sins and has paid the price for them, then they can also believe that He suffered for their healing and paid the price for it. It is just as much God's will to heal people as it is His will to forgive them of their sins.

The "Redemptive Chapter" of the Bible, Isaiah 53, was written in the later half of the eighth century B.C. and clearly describes the sufferings of the coming Messiah Who would redeem people from their sins and sickness.

He is despised, and left of men,
A man of pains, and acquainted with sickness,
And as one hiding the face from us,
He is despised, and we esteemed him not.
Surely our sicknesses he hath borne,
And our pains—he hath carried them,
And we—we have esteemed him plagued,
Smitten of God, and afflicted.
And he is pierced for our transgressions,
Bruised for our iniquities,
The chastisement *of our* peace is on him,
And by his bruise there is healing to us
(Is. 53:3-5 YLT Young's Literal Translation).

Jesus' suffering was not only for the redemption of people's transgressions and iniquities, but also for their physical healing. There are those who will say that the healing mentioned here is spiritual healing, not physical healing. However, this argument is contradicted by the following passage:

> When evening had come, they brought to him many who were demon-possessed. And He cast out the spirits with a word, and healed all who were sick, that it might be fulfilled which was spoken by Isaiah the prophet, saying:
>
> *"He himself took our infirmities*
> *And bore our sicknesses"* (Mat. 8:16-17).

These words confirm that Jesus took people's infirmities and bore (carried away) their diseases. If Jesus bore people's diseases for them, then they do not have to bear them themselves. This same passage from Isaiah is also quoted in 1 Peter:

> who Himself bore our sins in His own body on the tree, that we, having died to sins, might live for righteousness—by whose stripes you were healed (1 Peter 2:24).

Notice that Isaiah states, *there is healing to us,* while 1 Peter states, *you were healed.* This change in verb tense is quite significant. In the time intervening when these two passages were written, Jesus had suffered, died, and was raised from the dead. Therefore, this redemptive act has already provided for believers' healing just as it has already provided for their forgiveness of sins.

Another proof that healing is part of redemption comes to us in Paul's letter to the Galatians:

Christ has redeemed us from the curse of the law, having become a curse for us (for it is written, *"Cursed is everyone who hangs on a tree")* (Gal. 3:13),

As mentioned in Chapter One, the Curse of the Law is found in the book of Deuteronomy, part of the Pentateuch or what is known as "The Law."

But it shall come to pass, if you do not obey the voice of the Lord your God, to observe carefully all His commandments and His statues which I command you today, that all these curses will come upon you and overtake you:...The Lord will make the plague cling to you until He has consumed you from the land which you are going to possess. The Lord will strike *you* with consumption, with fever, with inflammation, with severe burning fever,...The Lord will strike you with the boils of Egypt, with tumors, with the scab and with the itch, from which you cannot be healed. The Lord will strike you with madness and blindness and confusion of heart (Deu. 28:15, 21-22, 27-28).

Virtually every disease known to mankind is included in the Curse of the Law. Thus according to Galatians, believers have been redeemed from their sicknesses. That is to say, Jesus paid the price for people's sicknesses so Satan has no right to lay diseases on them. It is up to individuals to claim their right to their healing through faith just as they claim their right to salvation through faith.

If physical healing is included in the redemptive act of Jesus on the cross, then it must be included in Holy Communion, which commemorates Jesus and His redemptive action. In the preparation for the exodus of the Israelites out of Egypt, the Lord spoke to Moses:

"Speak to all the congregation of Israel, saying: 'On the tenth *day* of this month every man shall take for himself a lamb, according to the house of *his* father, a lamb for a household...Your lamb shall be without blemish, a male of the first year...(Ex. 12:3, 5).

This lamb became know as the "Passover Lamb." Several times in the New Testament, Jesus is referred to as the Passover Lamb.

The next day John saw Jesus coming toward him, and said, "Behold! The Lamb of God who takes away the sin of the world" (John 1:29)!

knowing that you were not redeemed with corruptible things, *like* silver or gold, from your aimless conduct *received* by tradition from your fathers, but with the precious blood of Christ, as of a lamb without blemish and without spot (1 Peter 1:18-19).

Notice that Peter is referring to the Passover Lamb that was to be without blemish. Paul makes it very clear that Jesus is *the believer's* Passover Lamb.

For indeed Christ, our Passover, was sacrificed for us (1 Cor. 5:7).

So then, what is the significance of the Passover Lamb for believers today, and how does it relate to Holy Communion? The bread and wine of communion commemorate the body and blood of Jesus, respectively.

The cup of blessing which we bless, is it not the communion of the blood of Christ? The bread which we break, is it not the communion of the body of Christ? (1 Cor. 10:16).

Communion wine commemorates the blood of Jesus for the remission of sins.

Then He took the cup, and gave thanks, and gave *it* to them saying, "Drink from it, all of you. For this is My blood of the new covenant, which is shed for many for the remission of sins" (Mat. 26:27-28).

The Passover Lamb's blood was to save the very lives of the first-born of Israel:

'And they shall take *some* of the blood and put *it* on the two door posts and on the lintel of the houses where they eat it...' Now the blood shall be a sign for you on the houses where you *are*. And when I see the blood, I will pass over you; and the plague shall not be on you to destroy *you* when I strike the land of Egypt (Ex. 12:7, 13).

While the blood of the Passover Lamb saved the physical lives of the first born of Israel, the blood of Jesus saves believers from spiritual death thus giving them eternal life.

Communion bread commemorates the body of Jesus for physical healing.

> And as they were eating, Jesus took bread, blessed *it* and broke *it,* and gave it to the disciples and said, "Take, eat; this is My body" (Mat. 26:26).

Notice that Jesus did not articulate what the commemoration of his body was for. Since He did not do so, many have believed that it was also for the remission of sins and eternal life. However, there is a different significance of the Passover Lamb's body.

> Then they shall eat the flesh on that night; roasted in fire,… (Ex. 12:8).

So the Israelites were to eat the flesh of the Passover Lamb the night before the actual exodus. But again there is no indication of what the flesh was for. A hint of this comes from Psalm 105, which is a succinct account of the exodus from Egypt.

> He also brought them out with silver and gold,
> And *there was* none feeble among His tribes (Ps. 105:37).

The statement that there were *none feeble among His tribes* has tremendous significance. Estimates have been made that up to two million people migrated out of Egypt! These estimates are based on the census of adult males recorded in the first chapter of Deuteronomy. The population included men, women, and children; the young and the old; the healthy and the sick. In any population of two million people, it would be normal for a few hundred to die and a few hundred to be born in a few days' time. Many states in America have laws requiring that ambulances and medical personnel be on site for any gatherings of over a few hundred people—this in a time of modern medical practice and a generally healthy population.

Yet there is no mention of the Israelites leaving the feeble behind or burying the dead as they were force-marched across the desert and chased by Pharaoh's chariots through the parted waters of the Red Sea. This happening is perhaps the greatest healing miracle of the Bible. This miracle still doesn't say that these people were made supernaturally healthy by eating the flesh of the Passover Lamb; however, subsequent writings do imply this.

> For he who eats and drinks in an unworthy manner eats and drinks judgment to himself, not discerning the Lord's body. For this reason many *are* weak and sick among you, and many sleep (1 Cor. 11:29—30).

Here it is shown that defiling and not discerning the Lord's body, that is communion bread, resulted in sickness and death. If the Lord's body had been discerned then they would have likely been healed of their diseases. According to Isaiah 53 we are physically healed *by his bruise,* that is the physical punishment metered out on Jesus' body. By commemorating His body in Holy Communion, we are commemorating the punishment of His body by which we are healed. This confirms that physical healing is part of God's redemptive plan for mankind.

It is important, however, to understand that communion bread, *per se,* is not a cure-all for people's diseases, no more than taking communion wine will result in the forgiveness of their sins. It is a commemoration that honors Jesus and increases people's faith.

Summary

The most fundamental proof that it is God's will to heal all believers is that physical healing is part of the redemptive act of Jesus during his scourging. Jesus not only brought people's sins to the cross but He also brought their sicknesses. The punishment of Jesus' body (Isaiah 53), as it is commemorated in the Holy Communion bread, is the redeeming act for people's physical and mental healing.

The next chapter discusses three more ways to prove that it is Jesus' will to heal all believers.

Chapter Six
The Will of God to Heal: Part II

Then Jesus put out His hand and touched him,
saying "I am willing; be cleansed."

(Mat. 8:3)

The last chapter showed that Jesus not only brought mankind's sins to the cross, but He also brought their sicknesses, proving that it is His will to heal all believers. This chapter discusses three other proofs that it is absolutely God's will to heal everyone who comes to Him in faith.

God's Will to Heal Plainly Stated

God's will to heal is plainly stated in the Scriptures. As can be seen from the following passages, Jesus came to do the will of the Father.

"I can of Myself do nothing. As I hear, I judge; and My judgment is righteous, because I do not seek My own will but the will of the Father who sent Me (John 5:30).

then He said, *"Behold, I have come to do your will, O God"* (Heb.10:9).

It is also known from the Scriptures that Jesus went about healing the sick.

But when Jesus knew *it,* He withdrew from there; and great multitudes followed Him, and He healed them all (Mat. 12:15).

"how God anointed Jesus of Nazareth with the Holy Spirit and with power, who went about doing good and healing all who were oppressed by the devil, for God was with Him (Acts 10:38).

As shown in Chapter One, sickness is the work of the devil.

If Jesus came to do the will of the Father and Jesus went about healing the multitudes, then it is the will of the Father to heal people.

In another passage, Jesus states plainly that it is His will to heal.

And behold, a leper came and worshipped Him, saying, "Lord, if You are willing, You can make me clean." Then Jesus put out *His* hand and touched him, saying, "I am willing; be cleansed." And immediately his leprosy was cleansed (Mat. 8:2-3).

Many have taken this passage out of context and believe that one should always add "...if it be Your will" on the end of any prayer for healing. Since it is proven without doubt that it is His will to heal anyone who asks Him in faith, then it is not only pointless to say this but also it suggests a lack of faith. One would not think of saying to Jesus, "Lord, forgive me of my sin, if it be your will," since all believers know that it is the Lord's will to forgive them of their sins if they repent and ask Him in faith. In the case of the healing of the leper, Jesus is simply stating that it is His will to heal.

Forgiveness/Healing Side-by-Side

Believers can know for certain that when they die they will have eternal life in God's heaven.

These things I have written to you who believe in the name of the Son of God, that you may know that you have eternal life, and that you may *continue* to believe in the name of the Son of God (1 John 5:13).

How can believers know that they have eternal life? By reading the Bible and finding out the truth that it is God's will to forgive them of their sins and grant them eternal life through faith in Jesus. If believers know that they have eternal life through Jesus Christ than they should have no argument that it is God's will to forgive them of their sins.

Several times in the Bible, forgiveness and healing are mentioned in the same breath, in the same context.

Who forgives all your iniquities,
Who heals all your diseases (Ps. 103:3),

Heal me, O LORD, and I shall be healed;
Save me, and I shall be saved,
For You *are* my praise (Jer. 17:14).

But to you who fear My name
The Sun of Righteousness shall arise
With healing in His wings (Mal. 4:2);

And the prayer of faith will save the sick, and the Lord will raise him up. And if he has committed sins, he will be forgiven (James 5:15).

who Himself bore our sins in His own body on the tree, that we, having died to sins, might live for righteousness—by whose stripes you were healed (1 Peter 2:24).

"Which is easier, to say to the paralytic, *'Your* sins are forgiven you,' or to say, 'Arise, take up your bed and walk?' But that you may know that the Son of Man has power on earth to forgive sins"—He said to the paralytic, "I say to you, arise, take up your bed, and go your way to your house." And immediately he arose, took up the bed, and went out in the presence of them all, so that all were amazed and glorified God, saying, "We never saw *anything* like this" (Mark 2:9—12)!

In this latter passage, Jesus is equating His authority to forgive sins with His authority over sickness. This also shows His willingness to forgive sins and to heal.

Any reasonable person would not believe only the portion of these passages that deals with forgiveness of sins and reject the portion that deals with healing. They are spoken of side by side, and each portion is equally valid. Therefore if people believe that it is God's will to forgive them of their sins, then they must also believe that it is God's will to heal them and be free of sickness.

Reductio ad Absurdum

Reductio ad absurdum (reduce to an absurdity) is a logical test that can be used to prove that it is God's will to heal people. In the logical test of *reductio ad absurdum,* one disproves a proposition by showing that it leads to an absurdity when carried to its logical conclusion.

In this case one assumes that it is *not* God's will to heal people. If it is not God's will to heal people, then it must be God's will for them to be sick. If it is God's will for them to be sick, than it would be a sin to seek any healing, since this would be contrary to God's will. Therefore, people would be committing a sin by taking any medicine or seeking medical help. But since God is the source of all healing (Chapter One), than it would be a sin to seek what God has provided. This contradiction or absurdity shows that it cannot be God's will for anyone to be sick. Therefore the only logical conclusion is that it is God's will to heal anyone who comes to Him in faith.

There are misconceptions concerning the will of God to heal people.

Misconception:

"Maybe it's not God's will to heal <u>me</u>."

It is God's will to heal anyone who comes to Him in faith. People should never entertain the false notion that it might not be God's will to heal them. This notion comes from Satan, who wants people sick and to remain sick.

When Satan tempted Jesus during His forty-day fast, He always countered Satan with "It is written…" He would then go on to quote the Scriptures. People should study these last two Chapters over and over again until the Scriptures become ingrained in their thinking. When Satan tempts someone with the notion that it may not be God's will to heal him or her, than they should quote these Scripture back to him.

Many people's faith has increased by the revelation that it is God's will to heal them. They feel more peace and joy knowing that it is His will.

Misconception:

"Lord, heal me if it be Your will."

In many cases, when God's will in a matter is not known and not specifically revealed in the Scriptures, then it is appropriate to add to one's prayer, "…if it be Your will." However, when the will of God is plainly revealed in the Scriptures, it is pointless to say this and implies a lack of faith. It does not make sense for someone to pray earnestly for forgiveness and salvation and add "if it be Your will." Of course it is God's will to forgive and save people who come to Him in faith. That is why He sent His Son to be crucified. Likewise it does not make sense to add this to a prayer for healing, since it is God's will to heal.

Summary

As plainly stated in the Scriptures, it is absolutely God's will to heal anyone who comes to Him in faith. It is a logical absurdity to assume that it is not God's will to heal. Healing is just as much a part of the atonement as salvation. The Scriptures talk about salvation and physical healing in the same context. Therefore it is just as much His will to heal people of their diseases as it is His will to forgive them of their sins.

The next chapter discusses common misconceptions that people have about faith healing.

Chapter Seven
Common Questions Concerning God's Will to Heal

And you shall know the truth, and the truth shall make you free.

(John 8:32)

There are common questions concerning God's will to heal. People frequently voice these questions when the subject of faith healing is being discussed. The typical answers given to these questions are largely misconceived, thereby cheating countless thousands of people out of their healing. This Chapter discusses these questions the light of biblical truth.

Are Miracles and Healings for Today?

Misconceptions:

"The day of miracles is past."

"The healing that Christ did was only to show His deity. It is not for us today."

"The healing that the apostles and disciples did was a special power given by Jesus through the Holy Spirit in order to get the church started. This power died with the disciples."

It is informative to look at what is known as the Great Commission in the Gospel of Mark:

And he said to them, "Go into all the world and preach the gospel to every creature. He who believes and is baptized will be saved; but he who does not believe will be condemned. And these signs will follow those who believe: In My name they will cast out demons; they will speak with new tongues; they will take up serpents; and if they drink anything deadly, it will by no means hurt them; they will lay hands on the sick, and they will recover" (Mark 16:15-18).

Without question, the Great Commission to *go into the world and preach the gospel to every creature...* applies today. This is the reason missionaries are sent into the field and evangelists preach on the streets and in churches. But in the same Commission, Jesus said that...*they will lay hands on the sick and they will recover.* Therefore the laying of hands on the sick is just as valid today as preaching the Gospel to every creature.

In the first sentence Jesus is talking to *them.* It is known from verse 14 that Jesus was talking to His eleven disciples. Then why does Jesus use the third person to say *they will lay hands on the sick...?* The *they* that He is speaking of are those who believe and are baptized. This obviously includes everyone and anyone who believes today. If healing power was just for the disciples, then why didn't He say, "*You* will lay hands on the sick and they will recover"? The Great Commission, which includes the laying on of hands for the healing of the sick, is for everyone who believes: *And these signs shall follow those who believe.*

Jesus had a similar discussion with His disciples that is recorded in the Gospel of John.

"Most assuredly, I say to you, he who believes in Me, the works that I do he will do also; and greater *works* than these he will do, because I go to My Father (John 14:12).

Again Jesus is talking to His disciples but uses the third person indicating *anyone* who believes. Jesus is also saying that those who believe in Him will do greater works than He did, including His healing miracles. Believers will be able to do this because, He said, "I go to My Father." This statement applies to everyone who believes after Jesus' resurrection, and not just to His disciples.

It is true that at one time Jesus gave the power to heal specifically to His disciples.

And when He had called His twelve disciples to *Him,* He gave them power *over* unclean spirits, to cast them out, and to heal all kinds of sickness and all kinds of disease (Mat. 10:1).

However, this was given during His earthly ministry and is the reason that Jesus did not give this authority specifically to the disciples as part of the Great Commission—they already had the authority. Therefore the authority given as part of the Great Commission to heal was given to those coming after the disciples.

So when Peter saw *it,* he responded to the people: "Men of Israel, why do you marvel at this? Or why look so intently at us, as though by our own power or godliness we had made this man walk?...And His name, through faith in His name, has made this man strong, whom you see and know. Yes, the faith which *comes* through Him has given him this perfect soundness in the presence of you all (Acts 3:12, 16).

Notice that Peter did not say that a special anointing, given to him as an apostle by Jesus, healed this man. It was through faith that this man was healed, and the same faith is available to all believers for all time including the present.

It is also important to understand that Jesus does not change from generation to generation:

For I *am* the Lord, I do not change (Mal. 3:6);

...But the word of our God stands forever" (Is. 40:8 and quoted in 1 Peter 1:25).

Jesus Christ *is* the same yesterday, today, and forever (Heb. 13:8).

If Jesus healed yesterday, then He will heal today and tomorrow. It would be a contradiction to Hebrews 13:8 to say that Jesus would heal yesterday, but not today or tomorrow.

A non-biblical way to prove that it is God's will to heal today is the abundant evidence of countless faith healings that happen every day. These healings happen almost routinely in churches that believe in and practice the healing Gospel.

Is It God's Will to Heal Everyone and Specifically Me?

Misconceptions:

"God may heal others but He doesn't seem to want to heal me."

53

"Faith healing is just for those whom God happens to want to heal."

The notion that God picks and chooses those He wishes to heal, leaving others in their sickness, is a total contradiction to what is stated in the Scriptures. When Jesus went about healing, He healed *everyone* who came to Him for healing. There is no Scripture that shows that Jesus refused anyone's request for healing.

For everyone who asks receives…(Mat. 7:8),

When evening had come, they brought to Him many who were demon-possessed. And He cast out the spirits with a word, and healed all who were sick (Mat. 8:16),

But when Jesus knew *it*, He withdrew from there; and great multitudes followed Him, and He healed them all (Mat. 12:15).

And when Jesus went out He saw a great multitude; and He was moved with compassion for them, and healed their sick (Mat. 14:14).

Now when the sun was setting, all those who had anyone sick with various diseases brought them to Him; and He laid His hands on every one of them and healed them (Luke 4:40).

Also a multitude gathered from the surrounding cities to Jerusalem, bringing sick people and those who were tormented by unclean sprits, and they were all healed (Acts 5:16).

To say that Jesus will heal some people who ask but not all would be to say that Jesus picks and chooses those He wishes to heal. In other words, Jesus would be partial to some and not to others. However the Scriptures show this not to be the case.

Then Peter opened *his* mouth and said: "In truth I perceive that God shows no partiality" (Acts 10:34).

For there is no partiality with God (Rom. 2:11).

If God is not partial toward anyone than He is willing to heal everyone who asks Him in faith.

Can God Heal This Particular Disease?

Misconceptions:

"There is no way that God can possibly heal this disease."

"There is no way that God can make me whole again."

"I am too far gone to be healed."

With this kind of thinking, people typically abandon all hope for their healing because they question God's ability to heal their particular disease. Their disease is far too advanced or profound damage has already been afflicted on their bodies. God is omnipotent; there is nothing He cannot do. He formed the heavens and the earth with a word. This same God can restore bodies and eliminate diseases no matter how severe or devastating.

"Behold, I *am* the Lord, the God of all flesh. Is there anything too hard for Me" (Jer. 32:27)?

But Jesus looked at *them* and said to them, "With men this is impossible, but with God all things are possible" (Mat. 19:26).

For with God nothing will be impossible (Luke 1:37).

He did not waver at the promise of God through unbelief, but was strengthened in faith, giving glory to God, and being fully convinced that what He had promised He was also able to perform (Rom. 4:20-21).

It is absolutely within God's ability to heal and make anyone whole no matter what or how severe his or her condition may be, but some will think that even if they are healed of their disease they will be left with a body that is maimed or otherwise damaged. Maybe they have been injured in an accident where no disease is involved. Can God heal them?

Then great multitudes came to Him, having with them *those who were* lame, blind, mute, maimed, and many others; and they laid them down at Jesus' feet, and He healed them. So the multitude marveled when they saw *the* mute speaking, *the* maimed made whole, *the* lame walking, and *the* blind seeing; and they glorified the God of Israel (Mat. 15:30-31).

...*even* God, who gives life to the dead and calls those things which do not exist as though they did (Rom. 4:17);

God can and does make maimed bodies whole. God not only has the power to heal; he also has the power to create *those things which do not exist as though they did.* Women who have had hysterectomies have later naturally conceived and given birth to healthy babies—their reproductive organs being miraculously restored. Crippled and maimed bodies have been restored. There is nothing that God can not do.

God also heals mental illness.

For God has not given us a spirit of fear, but of power and of love and of a sound mind (2 Tim. 1:7).

If God has given people a sound mind, then mental illness is of Satan.

For whatever is born of God overcomes the world. And this is the victory that has overcome the world—our faith (1 John 5:4).

Here *the world* refers to Satan and his domain. Through faith believers have victory over Satan and his works—sin and sickness. Since believers have authority over him, mental illness must go as well.

Will God Heal this Particular Disease?

Misconceptions:

"I won't ask God to heal this because it is too trivial."

"How can I ask God to heal this when other people are dying of their diseases?"

People typically feel that what they are suffering from is trivial compared with other diseases, and so it would be imposing upon God to ask Him to heal them. The Scriptures are abundantly clear that God heals *all* diseases, both trivial and profound.

…Who heals all your diseases (Ps. 103.3),

Now Jesus went about all Galilee, teaching in their synagogues, preaching the gospel of the kingdom, and healing all kinds of sickness and all kinds of disease among the people (Mat. 4:23-24).

And when He had called His twelve disciples to *Him,* He gave them power *over* unclean spirits, to cast them out, and to heal all kinds of sickness and all kinds of disease (Mat. 10:1).

Thus if, Jesus healed *all kinds* of sickness and disease, then he healed both profound and trivial diseases. God wants to heal colds, bee stings, and annoying allergies. And He does so.

Am I Deserving of Healing?

Misconceptions:

"I do not deserve to be healed."

"I can't expect God to heal this because I am sinful."

"Faith healing is too good to be true."

"I am not lucky enough to be healed."

"I won't ask God to heal this because it is too much to expect."

All of these statements reflect a sentiment of unworthiness. They say, "I am not worthy to be healed." If people think that they are unworthy to be healed, they are absolutely right! They are no more worthy to be healed than they are to be forgiven of their sins. Faith healing, like salvation, is not a matter of worthiness, it is a gift of God that can not be earned but must be appropriated through faith.

The centurion answered and said, "Lord, I am not worthy that You should come under my roof. But only speak a word, and my servant will be healed. For I also am a man under authority, having soldiers under me. And I say to this *one,* 'Go,' and he goes; and to another, 'Come,' and he comes; and to my servant, 'Do this,' and he does *it.*" When Jesus heard *it,* he marveled, and said to those who followed, "Assuredly, I say to you, I have not found such great faith, not even in Israel" (Mat. 8:8-10)!

Jesus did not correct the centurion by telling him that he was worthy. He only saw his faith and went on to heal the servant.

If some are convicted by sin and that is keeping them away from faith healing, then it is most important that they go to the feet of Jesus, repent, and confess their sins:

If we confess our sins, He is faithful and just to forgive us *our* sins and to cleanse us from all unrighteousness (1 John 1:9).

then they can go to Him for healing. Remember that healing and forgiveness are mentioned side by side throughout the Scriptures.

Who forgives all your iniquities,
Who heals all your diseases (Ps. 103:3),

And the prayer of faith will save the sick, and the Lord will raise him up. And if he has committed sins, he will be forgiven (James 5:15).

who Himself bore our sins in his own body on the tree, that we, having died to sins, might live for righteousness—by whose stripes you were healed (1 Peter 2:24).

But isn't God sovereign?

Misconceptions:

"God is sovereign, and He can heal or not heal whoever He wills."

"That person is not healed because God is His sovereignty has decided not to heal him."

There is no argument that God is sovereign, and in His sovereignty He has decided to send His Son to suffer for mankind's healing as well as to die for their sins. One might argue, "God is sovereign, and He can forgive or not forgive anyone he wills," and go on to quote Jesus:

"But if you do not forgive men their trespasses, neither will your Father forgive your trespasses" (Mat. 6:15).

But there is a condition set here, *if you do not forgive.* The only condition set on healing is that one has faith in Jesus to perform what He has promised. The Lord has promised to heal anyone who asks Him in faith. He has made this promise out of His sovereignty. Therefore God's sovereignty should be viewed as supporting believer's faith, not undermining it.

Summary

The true biblical answers to common questions about faith healing give additional insight into God's will to heal.

Miracles and healing are for all times including the present and the future. Jesus Christ is the same yesterday, today and tomorrow.

It is God's will to heal everybody. God is not partial to anyone.

God is fully capable of healing any disease and restoring any bodily or mental condition. With God, nothing is impossible.

God is willing to heal any and all disease no matter how profound or trivial.

Healing does not depend on a person's worthiness, only on their faith.

God's sovereignty should be viewed as supporting believer's faith for healing, not undermining it.

The next chapter discusses the most misunderstood aspect of faith healing—God's timing for one's healing.

Chapter Eight
The Timing of God's Healing

"For assuredly, I say to you, whoever says to this mountain, 'Be removed and be cast into the sea,' and does not doubt in his heart but believes that those things he says will come to pass, he will have whatever he says.

(Mark 11:23)

God can and does heal in miraculous and instantaneous ways; however, in many cases it may take some time for the healing to manifest. People are called upon to not only have faith but patience, diligence, and endurance as well. It must be pointed out that medical healing may also require patience, diligence, and endurance, and only rarely will it be manifested instantaneously or miraculously.

This leads to one of the most confusing aspects of faith healing: that of God's timing in bringing about the healing. Most testimonies of faith healing emphasize the instantaneous, miraculous healings that are both startling and awe-inspiring. This kind of testimony can increase people's hope for their own healing, thereby helping to increase their faith. On the other hand, it can lead to a misconception that God only heals in miraculous and instantaneous ways.

This misconception frequently leads to the following line of thinking: "If I am not instantly healed, then I am probably not going to be healed. If I am not healed in a few days then I will likely not be healed. And, if I am not healed in a few weeks than I'll never be healed." Many have lost their healings because of this type of thinking, which usually causes them to abandon their faith in God to heal them.

A widely held myth is that every time Jesus laid hands on the sick or commanded disease leave there was always an instantaneous healing. According to the Scriptures, there were times when healings did not manifest until sometime later or were manifested gradually.

But Jesus turned around, and when He saw her He said, "Be of good cheer, daughter; your faith has made you well." And the woman was made well from that hour (Mat. 9:22).

Then Jesus answered and said to her, "O woman, great is your faith! let it be to you as you desire." And her daughter was healed from that very hour (Mat. 15:28).

And Jesus rebuked the demon, and it came out of him; and the child was cured from that very hour (Mat. 17:18).

Then as He entered a certain village, there met Him ten men who were lepers, who stood afar off. And they lifted up *their* voices and said, "Jesus, Master, have mercy on us!" So when He saw *them*, He said to them, "Go, show yourselves to the priests." And so it was that as they went, they were cleaned (Luke 17:12—14).

When He had said these things, he spat on the ground and made clay with the saliva; and He anointed the eyes of the blind man with the clay. And He said to him, "Go, wash in the pool of Siloam" (which is translated, Sent). So he went and washed, and came back seeing (John 9:6—7).

In all these cases Jesus decided to heal the people gradually or some time later, not instantly. If there is any area in healing where God exercises His sovereign authority, it is in the area of timing. There is nothing in the Scriptures that say that God only heals instantly. In one Bible verse Jesus says that it may take time to get what one is praying for with faith:

"For assuredly, I say to you, whoever says to this mountain, 'Be removed and be cast into the sea,' and does not doubt in his heart but believes that those things he says will come to pass, he will have whatever he says (Mark 11:23).

Notice the verb tense of the phrase *will come to pass.* Its future tense obviously states that some time will pass before whatever one is praying for is manifested.

The Scriptures teach us to have *patience.*

that you do not become sluggish, but imitate those who through faith and patience inherit the promises (Heb. 6:12).

Healing is a promise of God to those who ask Him in faith. But now we see that patience may also be required, and not just patience where people sit around doing nothing waiting for God to heal them—they also need to exercise diligence.

But without faith *it is* impossible to please *Him*, for he who comes to God must believe that He is, and *that* he is a rewarder of those who diligently seek Him (Heb. 11:6).

Another quote from the Scriptures further implies the need for diligence.

Ask, and it will be given to you; seek, and you will find; knock, and it will be opened to you. For everyone who asks receives, and he who seeks finds, and to him who knocks it will be opened (Mat. 7:7-8).

Here the message is to *keep on seeking* and *keep on knocking*. This means diligence. People must be diligent in seeking Him for their healing. In medical healing people can be diligent by taking their medication and following their doctors' instructions, but what are people to do for faith healing? These things are discussed in the next two chapters.

My brethren, count it all joy when you fall into various trials, knowing that the testing of your faith produces patience. But let patience have *its* perfect work, that you may be perfect and complete, lacking nothing (James 1:2-4).

Disease and suffering can certainly test people's faith. When people go to a medical doctor with an infection and the doctor prescribes an antibiotic, they generally do not think that they will be healed instantly after taking the first pill. The doctor may have told them to keep on taking the pills for two weeks. So what do they do when after two weeks they are still sick? They go back to the doctor who may then prescribe some other kind of antibiotic. If this goes on for several weeks or even months people inevitably start to lose faith in the doctor. They may even go to another doctor. The same kind of thing can happen with faith healing. If they are not healed quickly they may start to lose faith for their healing. They must have *endurance*.

65

Therefore do not cast away your confidence, which has great reward. For you have need of endurance, so that after you have done the will of God, you may receive the promise (Heb. 10:35—36):

Many times people who have been gravely sick for months or years are instantaneously and miraculously healed by the power of God. In other cases the healing may manifest gradually over a period of time. Many others are healed in minutes, hours, days, and sometimes months, but in all cases they are healed by the power of God through faith. It is not at all uncommon for those in the healing ministry to lay hands on the sick with no apparent result only to find out later that they were healed the next day or within a few hours after having hands laid on them.

There is a common misconception concerning the timing of God's healing.

Misconception:

"I've had hands laid on me several times, and I'm still not healed."

Another myth about Jesus is that people were healed the first time He laid hands on them. But the Gospel of Mark shows that this is not so.

So He took the blind man by the hand and led him out of the town. And when He had spit on his eyes and put His hands on him, He asked him if he saw anything. And he looked up and said, "I see men like trees, walking." Then He put *His* hands on his eyes again and made him look up. And he was restored and saw everyone clearly (Mark 8:23-25).

Jesus was and is the Christ, the Anointed One, yet He laid hands on the blind man twice. Why? Because of the unbelief of those around Him. Jesus had just scolded His disciples for their lack of faith. Mark says that Jesus led the man out of town before laying hands on him. This was probably to get away from the unbelief among the people.

And He did not do many mighty works there because of their unbelief (Mat. 13:58).

There in this case was while Jesus was in "His own country" (Mat. 13:54). This passage does not say that Jesus *could* not, it says He *did* not. Unbelief is a sure way to slow down or even prevent the manifestation of one's healing. The statement "and I am still not healed," while being a statement of fact, is a confession of lack of faith. Faith would say, "and I am healed by the stripes of Jesus."

Summary

God can and does heal in miraculous and instantaneous ways. In other cases it may take some time for the healing to manifest. There are many cases in which people are called to have not only faith but patience, diligence, and endurance as well. Unbelief is a sure way to slow down the manifestation of one's healing.

The next two chapters discuss ways in which people can diligently maintain and build their faith for healing.

Chapter Nine
Proper Attitudes of the Heart and Mind

But to you who fear My name
The Sun of Righteousness shall arise
With healing in His wings;...

(Mal. 4:2)

Hebrews 6:12 teaches that believers "inherit the promises" through "faith *and* patience." Believers may be called upon not only to have faith for their healing but to have patience, diligence, and endurance as well. One reason people may have to wait for their healing is that their faith may not be fully developed. In order to have endurance they must diligently foster their faith. "Foster" means to promote the growth or development of something, in this case their faith for healing.

There are two areas in which people can foster their faith. The first is to develop proper attitudes in their hearts and minds, which will be discussed in this chapter. The second is to take appropriate action. Appropriate action will be covered in the next chapter.

The Scriptures reveal several attitudes that foster faith for healing and may actually bring about healing.

Fear (reverence, awe) of God

The word *fear* in the following verses means reverence and awe of God.

Do not be wise in your own eyes;
Fear the Lord and depart from evil.
It will be health to your flesh,
And strength to your bones (Pr. 3:7-8).

But to you who fear My name
The Sun of Righteousness shall arise
With healing in His wings...(Mal. 4:2);

These Scriptures say that reverence and awe of God brings healing! People who want to be healed must have reverence for God. They must not use His name casually or profanely. Jesus must be the Lord of their lives.

Therefore God also has highly exalted Him and given Him the name which is above every name that at the name of Jesus every knee should bow, of those in heaven, and of those on earth, and of those under the earth, and *that* every tongue should confess that Jesus Christ *is* Lord, to the glory of God the Father (Phil. 2:9-11).

People should examine their attitude toward Jesus. Jesus can be their personal friend and confidant, but He is also Almighty God, Creator of the Universe. In other words He is both Lamb and Lion.

Trust in the Lord

One of greatest insults that people can commit against the Lord is to not trust Him. Trust is something that comes from faith. If one has faith in someone, they trust him. To say that someone has faith in God to heal him or her but doesn't really trust Him to do so is a contradiction. Since God and His Word are inseparable, one must also trust God's Word, the Bible.

Trust in the Lord with all your heart,
And lean not on your own understanding (Pr. 3:5);

Trust in the Lord, and do good;
Dwell in the land, and feed on His faithfulness.
Delight yourself also in the Lord,
And he shall give you the desires of your heart
(Ps. 37:3-4).

If it is the desire of one's heart to be healed, then that person must trust in the Lord to heal him. It is His will and His promise to do so.

The Lord *is* good,
A stronghold in the day of trouble;
And He knows those who trust in Him (Nahum 1:7).

The onslaught of sickness or infirmities can certainly be considered a *day of trouble.* Isn't it comforting to realize that the Lord knows and hears people when they trust Him to heal them?

Confidence in the Lord

Therefore do not cast away your confidence, which has great reward (Heb. 10:35).

Confidence is almost synonymous with trust. If people trust someone, they have confidence in him. Confidence also implies that the people believe that the person is capable of doing what he has promised to do. In discussing Abraham's faith, Paul writes:

> He did not waver at the promise of God through unbelief, but was strengthened in faith, giving glory to God, and being fully convinced that what He had promised He was also able to perform (Rom. 4:20-21).

Abraham's confidence in God to perform what He had promised was instrumental in strengthening of his faith. God's promise is to heal anyone who asks Him in faith. People can have confidence knowing that God is both willing and able to heal them.

Righteousness

Righteousness is freedom from guilt or sin. It is far more important to seek after righteousness than it is to seek after healing, but the Scriptures teach that seeking after righteousness also brings about healing.

> Do not be wise in your own eyes;
> Fear the Lord and depart from evil.
> It will be health to your flesh,
> And strength to your bones (Pr. 3:7-8).

> Afterward Jesus found him in the temple, and said to him, "See, you have been made well. Sin no more, lest a worse thing come upon you" (John 5:14).

How can people obtain righteousness? By repenting of their sins and seeking Jesus for forgiveness through faith.

If we confess our sins, He is faithful and just to forgive us *our* sins and to cleanse us from all unrighteousness (1 John 1:9).

For He made Him who knew no sin *to be* sin for us, that we might become the righteousness of God in Him (2 Cor. 5:21).

even the righteousness of God *which is* through faith in Jesus Christ to all and on all who believe (Rom. 3:22).

If people are convicted of sin in their life, they must repent and go to Jesus with faith for forgiveness. Then they can go to Him for the healing of their bodies.

Forgiveness

Therefore I say to you, whatever things you ask when you pray, believe that you receive *them*, and you will have *them.* And whenever you stand praying, if you have anything against anyone, forgive him, that your Father in heaven may also forgive you your trespasses (Mark 11:24-25).

Thus if people are asking God for healing but harbor some unforgiveness, then their prayers may not be effective. Indeed some illnesses seem to be directly related to unforgiveness.

Many people are confused as to just what forgiveness is. Some say that it is wishing well of someone who has wronged them. Others say that forgiveness is forgetting some wrong made against them. These sentiments are more the results of forgiveness, not forgiveness itself.

Forgiveness actually means to remove any claim one may have on a person who has done wrong to him. Forgiveness says that the offending person owes nothing: no apologies, no amends. Thus forgiveness is a conscious, willful freeing of any debt that an offending person may owe. After all, isn't that exactly what Jesus does when He forgives people of their sins? When they sin, they have a debt to pay to God. Jesus has already paid that debt on the cross, thus believers no longer have to pay for it in hell.

Forgiveness may be very difficult to do, but Jesus commands believers to do it, and their healing may likely depend upon it.

> For if you forgive men their trespasses, your heavenly Father will also forgive you. But if you do not forgive men their trespasses, neither will your Father forgive your trespasses (Mat. 6:14-15).

Knowledge of God's Will

It is imperative that people know that it is God's will to heal them. Otherwise it would be difficult if not impossible to have faith for their healing;

> For this reason we also, since the day we heard it, do not cease to pray for you, and to ask that you may be filled with the knowledge of His will in all wisdom and spiritual understanding (Col. 1:9);

> Now this is the confidence that we have in Him, that if we ask anything according to His will, He hears us. And if we know that He hears us, whatever we ask, we know that we have the petitions that we have asked of Him (1 John 5:14-15).

Chapter Four showed that the only way to know God's will is to read His word, the Bible.

A Merry Heart

In modern times, some individuals have promoted the healing nature of happiness or merriment. Indeed modern medical science has confirmed this to be true; however, the Scriptures had already pointed this out thousands of years ago.

A merry heart does good, *like* medicine,
But a broken spirit dries the bones (Pr. 17:22).

Furthermore the Scriptures point out that even pleasant words can have a healing effect.

Pleasant words *are like* a honeycomb,
Sweetness to the soul and health to the bones (Pr. 16:24).

How can people maintain a *merry heart* and *pleasant words* during the ravages of illness or infirmities? By having faith that Jesus will heal them. Chapter Three pointed out that peace and joy, the gifts of the Spirit are the results of true faith. Yes, faith will give the ability to maintain a merry heart throughout one's healing. And a merry heart itself brings about healing.

Summary

People must diligently foster their faith to have endurance. The Scriptures show that one way to foster their faith for healing is to develop proper attitudes in their hearts and minds. These include:

- reverence and awe of God
- trust in the Lord
- confidence in the Lord
- righteousness
- forgiveness
- knowledge of God's will
- a merry heart.

These attitudes actually bring about healing.

Chapter Ten
Appropriate Action

But be doers of the word, and not hearers only, deceiving yourselves.

(James 1:22)

The second way to foster one's faith for healing is to take appropriate action. Jesus Himself tells believers to take action based on their faith.

"Ask, and it will be given to you; seek, and you will find; knock, and it will be opened to you. For everyone who asks receives, and he who seeks finds, and to him who knocks it will be opened" (Mat. 7:7-8).

Asking, seeking, and *knocking* are all actions that one can take when requesting something from God.

It is very important to understand that action or works cannot and will not, by themselves, bring about people's salvation or their healing.

For by grace you have been saved through faith, and that not of yourselves; *it is* the gift of God, not of works, lest anyone should boast (Eph. 2:8-9).

In regard to healing, Jesus further makes this point.

for she said to herself, "If only I may touch His garment, I shall be made well." But Jesus turned around, and when He saw her He said, "Be of good cheer, daughter; your faith has made you well." And the women was made well from that hour (Mat. 9:21-22).

Many have thought, "If only Jesus were here now in the flesh, I would touch His garment and be healed," but notice that it was not her action of touching Jesus' garment, it was her faith demonstrated by her action. Therefore this lady had no opportunity better than every believer today who has faith.

Works, such as feeding the hungry, are things that believers do because of their faith. Indeed performing these works can and will increase people's faith; however, there is a great danger here. Some may unconsciously start to believe that by doing them they will somehow earn their healing. "You see how hard I am working? Now God will have to heal me."

Some people believe that by doing these acts of faith, they will somehow change or influence God's will to heal them. God has already done everything he has to do for their healing, and it is entirely His will to do so. It is useless and unnecessary for people to try to change God's mind about their healing since it is already God's will to heal them and God does not change.

For I *am* the Lord, I do not change (Mal. 3:6);

The only thing people need to do in order to receive their healing is to have faith in Jesus' will to heal them. Also, the Lord hears people when they ask Him to heal them, so they do not have to get His attention.

Now this is the confidence that we have in Him, that if we ask anything according to His will, He hears us (1 John 5:14).

Therefore people cannot affect God's will for their healing by taking action; they are really affecting their own faith. They are fostering their faith for healing.

In every example of healing in the Gospels, the person being healed took some form of action.

When He had said these things, He spat on the ground and made clay with the saliva; and He anointed the eyes of the blind man with the clay. And He said to him, "Go, wash in the pool of Siloam" (which is translated, Sent). So he went and washed, and came back seeing (John 9:6-7).

And Elisha sent a messenger to him, saying, "Go and wash in the Jordan seven times, and your flesh shall be restored to you, and *you shall* be clean."...So he went down and dipped seven times in the Jordan, according to the saying of the man of God; and his flesh was restored like the flesh of a little child, and he was clean (2 Kings 5:10, 14).

At this point some may be thinking: "If the Lord told me to do something for my healing I would certainly do it. If He told me to dip seven times in a river in the middle of winter, I would do it and be done with it." Thankfully, the Lord has made action for healing much easier than that.

Ask the Father in Jesus' Name

Jesus repeatedly told people to ask the Father in His name for the things they need.

"And whatever you ask in My name, that I will do, that the Father may be glorified in the Son. If you ask anything in My name I will do *it*" (John 14:13-14).

This passage states that, by asking the Father in Jesus' name to heal them, people actually give Jesus an opportunity to bring glory to the Father. Of course Jesus wants to bring glory to the Father by healing those who ask.

"If you abide in Me, and My words abide in you, you will ask what you desire, and it shall be done for you (John 15:7).

"...Most assuredly, I say to you, whatever you ask the Father in My name He will give you. Until now you have asked nothing in My name. Ask, and you will receive, that your joy may be full" (John 16:23-24).

"Ask, and it will be given to you...For everyone who asks receives" (Mat. 7:7-8),

"If you then, being evil, know how to give good gifts to your children, how much more will your Father who is in heaven give good things to those who ask Him (Mat. 7:11)!

"Again I say to you that if two of you agree on earth concerning anything that they ask, it will be done for them by My Father in heaven (Mat. 18:19).

Notice that Jesus is urging believers to simply *ask*. He did not tell them to bargain, beg, coax, flatter, or threaten. Asking implies faith. One would not simply ask God if they did not believe He would, could, and willed to heal them. On the other hand, bargaining or begging is a sure indication that one does not have the necessary faith to be healed. Such carrying on does not manifest healing, only faith does.

> Now this is the confidence that we have in Him, that if we ask anything according to His will, He hears us (1 John 5:14).

Here John adds the provision *according* to *His will*. Since it is absolutely God's will to heal anyone who asks him in faith, one can ask Him with confidence for their healing. John also says *He hears us*, so repetitious asking is unnecessary and would be equivalent to begging. This is not to say that people should stop praying after they ask the Father in Jesus' name to heal them. Instead their constant prayer after asking should be one of praise and thanksgiving.

> Rejoice always, pray without ceasing, in everything give thanks; for this is the will of God in Christ Jesus for you (1 Thes. 5:16-18).

If one hasn't already done so, he or she should now simply ask the Father in Jesus' name to heal them.

Believe That God Will Heal

Believing is the essence of faith.

> Jesus said to him, "If you can believe, all things are possible to him who believes" (Mark 9:23).

Therefore I say to you, whatever things you ask when you pray, believe that you receive *them* and you will have *them* (Mark 11:24).

Jesus said to him, "Go your way; your son lives." So the man believed the word that Jesus spoke to him, and he went his way. And as he was now going down, his servants met him and told *him*, saying, "Your son lives" (John 4:50-51)!

Believing is an action. It is something people make a conscious decision to do. They can believe that Jesus will heal them or not believe it, the choice is theirs.

Speak Healing

"For assuredly, I say to you, whoever says to this mountain, 'Be removed and be cast into the sea,' and does not doubt in his heart, but believes that those things he says will come to pass, he will have whatever he says" (Mark 11:23).

Believers should speak healing to their minds and bodies. They should command sickness to leave in the name of Jesus. Constantly saying and believing that they are healed even though they are still suffering is a powerful way for people to foster their faith. Faith says they are already healed. They walk by faith not by sight.

Death and life *are* in the power of the tongue,
And those who love it will eat its fruit (Pr. 18:21).

People who need healing should not habitually go around telling people how much they are suffering. They should also not keep telling themselves how bad off they are. This kind of testimony gives Satan the glory for what he has done to them. It also conditions them to accept their sickness, which is clearly contrary to faith.

This does not mean that they should not be open about their actual condition when speaking to a doctor or to someone administering intercessory faith healing. This will not violate faith. Fear of speaking to a doctor or intercessor will make it difficult to properly prescribe medication or to effectively pray for healing. The important thing is not to make a habit of such speech.

Whenever people's sickness gets the best of them, they should start praising God for their healing. A good way to do this is to quote out loud a favorite paraphrased healing verse. For example:

By the stripes of Jesus, I am healed! (Is. 53:5).

I am redeemed from the curse of the Law and that includes this disease! (Gal.3:13).

Jesus has forgiven my sins and has healed this disease! (Ps. 103:3).

Thank the Father

The apostle Paul admonishes believers to always thank the Father in Jesus' name.

giving thanks always for all things to God the Father in the name of our Lord Jesus Christ (Eph. 5:20).

Rejoice always, pray without ceasing, in everything give thanks; for this is the will of God in Christ Jesus for you (1 Thes. 5:16-18).

Be anxious for nothing, but in everything by prayer and supplication, with thanksgiving, let your requests be made known to God (Phil. 4:6);

In the last verse, Paul further says to give God thanks even when asking for something. This means that believers are to thank the Father in Jesus' name for their healing when they ask Him, *before* it is actually manifested. This is entirely consistent with the definition of faith that says one firmly believes that he or she is already healed before it is manifested. The Bible records an example where thanksgiving actually brought about healing.

Leprosy was and is a horrible bacterial disease. It produces sores and lumps accompanied by the loss of feelings, the wasting away of muscle, and the production of deformities and mutilations. In the Bible, to be *cleansed* of leprosy meant that disease was stopped and the sores healed; the person was still left with the effects of the disease: deformities and mutilations. To be made *whole* meant that the deformities and mutilations were reconstructed and the body restored to normal. This distinction is made clear by the healing of Naaman in Second Kings:

So he went down and dipped seven times in the Jordan, according to the saying of the man of God; and his flesh was restored like the flesh of a little child, and he was clean (2 Kings 5:14).

Healing of leprosy that Jesus performed during His earthly ministry shows how *thanksgiving* brought about healing.

> And as he entered into a certain village, there met him ten men that were lepers, which stood afar off: And they lifted up *their* voices, and said, Jesus, Master, have mercy on us. And when he saw *them*, he said unto them, Go shew yourselves unto the priests. And it came to pass, that, as they went, they were cleansed. And one of them, when he saw that he was healed, turned back, and with a loud voice glorified God, And fell down on *his* face at his feet, giving him thanks: and he was a Samaritan. And Jesus answering said, Were there not ten cleansed? but where *are* the nine? There are not found that returned to give glory to God, save this stranger. And he said unto him, Arise, go thy way: thy faith hath made thee whole (Luke 17:12-19 AV).

Thus by giving Jesus his thanks, the Samaritan was not only cleansed but was also made whole. The other nine lepers had been cleansed but were left with their deformities and mutilations.

The message here is that people should give thanks for their healing before and after it is manifested.

Cast Out the Spirit of Disease in Jesus' Name

The first chapter showed that Satan is the source of all disease and Jesus is the source of all healing. Therefore it is understandable that certain diseases and conditions are the direct result of satanic influence.[1] Satanic or demonic influence

---

[1] This is satanic *influence* as opposed to demonic *possession.* Demonic possession is very real and is devastating, but exorcism is not the subject of this book.

in sickness can be illustrated by the following Scriptural example.

> And behold, there was a woman who had a spirit of infirmity eighteen years, and was bent over and could in no way raise *herself* up. But when Jesus saw her, He called *her* to *Him* and said to her, "Woman, you are loosed from your infirmity." And He laid *His* hands on her, and immediately she was made straight, and glorified God (Luke 13:11-13).

Some may be thinking, "If spirit of infirmity has caused my disease how can medicine or faith heal me?" They will be happy to know God has given believers authority over these spirits.

> "Behold, I give you the authority to trample on serpents and scorpions, and over all the power of the enemy, and nothing shall by any means hurt you" (Luke 10:19).

Here the terms *serpents* and *scorpions* are symbolic references to evil spirits, and the word *enemy* refers to Satan. Some may argue that Jesus is talking to his disciples and that this power does not apply to believers today. This is not true since John makes a similar declaration in his first epistle.

> You are of God, little children, and have overcome them, because He who is in you is greater than he who is in the world (1 John 4:4).

The *you* that John is addressing here are the followers and believers of Christ Jesus, not the apostles. *He who is in you* refers to the Holy Spirit, and *he who is in the world* is Satan.

Thus, by the power of the Holy Spirit, believers have power over Satan. But how do believers exercise this power? By casting the evil spirits out in the name of Jesus.

And these signs will follow those who believe:
In My name they will cast out demons (Mark 16:17);

Casting out evil spirits of sickness in the name of Jesus is very simple and very effective. To cast out a disease one should say something such as, "You unclean spirit of [name the disease or condition], in the name of Jesus and with the power of the Holy Spirit, I command you out of my body." As believers with faith, people have this authority. They should use it.

Read the Word of God, the Bible

Chapter Four explained the importance of reading God's Word, the Bible, in order to build faith.

So then faith *comes* by hearing, and hearing by the word of God (Rom. 10:17).

Now people can look again at the reading of God's Word as a means of fostering their faith for healing. Several passages show that the reading of God's Word can bring about healing.

He sent His word and healed them
And delivered *them* from their destructions (Ps. 107:20).

Hear, my son, and receive my sayings,
And the years of your life will be many (Pr. 4:10),

My son, give attention to my words;
Incline your ear to my sayings.
Do not let them depart from your eyes;
Keep them in the midst of your heart;
For they *are* life to those who find them,
And health to all their flesh (Pr. 4:20-22).

Everyone should read the Bible. They should read it continuously and habitually. When people receive a letter from someone they love, they read it over and over again. The Bible is a collection of personal love letters from God to His people. They tell humans how much God loves them and wants them healed both spiritually and physically. Jesus has paid the price for both.

Pray for and Give Care to Others

Another way people can foster their faith for healing is to pray for and give care to others.

Is it not to share your bread with the hungry,
And that you bring to your house the poor who are cast out;
When you see the naked, that you cover him,
And not hide yourself from your own flesh?
Then your light shall break forth like the morning,
Your healing shall spring forth speedily (Is. 58:7-8).

Confess *your* trespasses to one another, and pray for one another, that you may be healed (James 5:16).

Caring for others is entirely consistent with the teachings of Jesus—namely, to put others ahead of themselves even in the times of their own needs.

"So the last will be first, and the first last" (Mat. 20:16).

Some may not be able to do much for other people because of their condition but they can always *pray* for other people. They should pray for others who are sick to be healed and expect them to be healed.

Take Communion Discerning the Body of Christ

Communion bread commemorates the body of Jesus. Chapter Five showed that its significance is for the healing of believers' bodies.

For he who eats and drinks in an unworthy manner eats and drinks judgment to himself, not discerning the Lord's body. For this reason many *are* weak and sick among you, and many sleep (1 Cor. 11:29-30).

Believers should take Communion often, and while they receive the bread thank Jesus for the suffering His body went through for their healing.

And by His stripes we are healed (Is. 53:5).

Seek Intercessory Faith Healing

The Scriptures teach believers to seek out intercessory faith healing. A serious disease can exhaust the sufferer and those around him, thus making it difficult for them to have the faith to be healed. God has provided intercessory faith to help people appropriate their healing. In this type of healing someone joins together with other people who have strong appropriating faith.

"Again I say to you that if two of you agree on earth concerning anything that they ask, it will be done for them by My Father in heaven" (Mat. 18:19).

Thus if the sick person can find someone with strong faith for healing they *can* both agree on his or her healing and then both can ask the Father in Jesus' name. Jesus has promised that *it will be done.*
There are many healing ministries where individuals have received the *gifts of healing* through faith.

...to another gifts of healings by the same Spirit
(1 Cor. 12:9),

"And these signs will follow those who believe:
...they will lay hands on the sick, and they will recover"
(Mark 16:17, 18).

People should seek out these ministries and have these individuals lay hands on them in the name of Jesus.

Another action involving intercessory faith healing is for sick people to ask their church elders to pray for them and to anoint them with oil.

Is anyone among you sick? Let him call for the elders of the church, and let them pray over him, anointing him with oil in the name of the Lord. And the prayer of faith will save the sick, and the Lord will raise him up (James 5:14-15).

Notice that this does not say that the sick are to wait until their church has a healing service where elders anoint with oil.

When people are sick they should call for the elders to pray over them and anoint them with oil in the name of Jesus. This would certainly be an act of faith.

There is a major misconception concerning appropriate action for healing.

Misconception:

"I can earn my healing by performing all of these actions."

Once again, people cannot earn their healing. Healing is a gift of God appropriated through faith. By doing these actions one is simply exercising and fostering their faith which will bring about their healing.

Summary

The Scriptures teach believers to take appropriate action as a natural outgrowth of their faith. Appropriate action for healing includes the following:

- ask the Father in Jesus' name for healing
- believe that He will heal
- speak healing, not sickness
- thank the Father for healing before and after it is manifested.
- cast out the spirit of disease in Jesus' Name
- read the Word of God, the Bible
- pray for and give care to others
- take communion discerning the Body of Christ
- seek intercessory faith healing.

People cannot earn their healing. Healing is a gift of God appropriated through faith.

The next chapter will look at the enemies of faith and healing.

Chapter Eleven
The Enemies of Faith and Healing

But let him ask in faith, with no doubting, for he who doubts is like a wave of the sea driven and tossed by the wind. For let not that man suppose that he will receive anything from the Lord.

(James 1:6-7)

In the previous chapters, only those things that build and foster faith have been discussed. Looking at negative things is also instructive, for they can reveal where a problem may lie if someone's healing is not manifested. This chapter discusses those attitudes and actions that are contrary to faith. Harboring any of these will undermine people's faith for their healing.

Fear and Worry

Fear and worry are common reactions to a disease or condition that is life-threatening or will prevent people from carrying out their normal activities. Many people with life-threatening diseases quickly develop fear and worry, as do their loved ones who surround them. However, Jesus admonishes people not to fear or worry.

"Look at the birds of the air, for they neither sow nor reap nor gather into barns; yet your heavenly Father feeds them. Are you not of more value than they? Which of you by worrying can add one cubit to his stature" (Mat. 6:26-27)?

Jesus Himself is saying that worrying is useless. Worrying also indicates that people do not trust God to heal them. But what does Jesus say about fear?

While He was still speaking, *some* came from the ruler of the synagogue's *house* who said, "Your daughter is dead. Why trouble the Teacher any further?" As soon as Jesus heard the word that was spoken, He said to the ruler of the synagogue, "Do not be afraid; only believe" (Mark 5:35-36).

The ruler of the synagogue's daughter was dead yet Jesus said, "Do not be afraid." Jesus was not being insensitive. He simply told him to believe, that is, to have faith. Jesus went on to raise his daughter from the dead.

And a great windstorm arose, and the waves beat into the boat, so that it was already filling. But He was in the stern, asleep on a pillow. And they awoke Him and said to Him, "Teacher, do You not care that we are perishing?" Then He arose and rebuked the wind, and said to the sea, "Peace, be still!" and the wind ceased and there was a great calm. But He said to them, "Why are you so fearful? How is *it* that you have no faith" (Mark 4:37-40)?

What was Jesus saying? If people are fearful, then they do not have faith. There is no room for fear in faith. People choose either to believe Jesus for their healing or to fear that He will not heal them. Also, the disciples said, "Teacher, do You not care that we are perishing?" Many have thought or said "Jesus, do You not care that I am dying from this disease?" Jesus says to them, "Faith will tell you that I care enough to heal you."

But isn't fear a natural, God-given emotion? The answer is no. How can God give someone an emotion that is contrary to faith?

For God has not given us a spirit of fear, but of power and of love and of a sound mind (2 Tim. 1:7).

God did not give humanity a spirit of fear, Satan did. Satan, who wants people sick, is the source of people's fear. What better way to undermine a person's faith?

If people's sickness makes them fear, they are not believing or trusting Jesus for their healing. This is simply stating the facts given by Jesus Himself. If Jesus commanded believers not to be afraid, then they have control over fear. Fear is an enemy. Believers can and should command the spirit of fear out of them in the name of Jesus. They will know that they have faith when all fear is gone. Fear displaces faith, but faith displaces fear. Faith is stronger than fear.

Doubt and Unbelief

Doubt and unbelief are the direct opposite of faith.

But let him ask in faith, with no doubting, for he who doubts is like a wave of the sea driven and tossed by the wind. For let not that man suppose that he will receive anything from the Lord (James 1:6-7);

And Peter answered Him and said, "Lord, if it is You, command me to come to You on the water." So He said, "Come." And when Peter had come down out of the boat, he walked on the water to go to Jesus. But when he saw that the wind *was* boisterous, he was afraid; and beginning to sink he cried out, saying, "Lord, save me!" And immediately Jesus stretched out *His* hand and caught him and said to him, "O you of little faith, why did you doubt" (Mat. 14:28-31)?

Believing is something one chooses to do. Doubt and unbelief are indications that one has chosen not to believe the Word of God.

And He did not do many mighty works there because of their unbelief (Mat. 13:58).

This Scripture does not say that Jesus *could not* do mighty works there, it says He *did not*. It is not that God is unable since God can do anything He wishes. It is simply that God demands and expects faith from His people. Why should God honor people's request for healing if they don't believe Him for it?

Dependence on Physical Senses

Chapter Three discussed the meaning and importance of faith.

Now faith is the substance of things hoped for, the evidence of things not seen (Heb. 11:1).

This biblical definition of faith includes the phrase of *things not seen.* Therefore faith does not depend on what one sees, feels, or experiences, the symptoms of his or her disease included. In other words, people must not look at their symptoms and say they are not being healed. This type of evidence has no place in faith; faith in the Word of God is the evidence. The Scriptures repeat this point several times.

For we walk by faith, not by sight (2 Cor. 5:7).

Then Jesus said to him, "Unless you *people* see signs and wonders, you will by no means believe" (John 4:48).

Jesus said to him, "Thomas, because you have seen Me, you have believed. Blessed *are* those who have not seen and *yet* have believed" (John 20:29).

People's symptoms indicate they are sick. The Word of God says they are healed. Faith says they believe the Word of God and not the symptoms. Oh yes, the symptoms are there screaming that they are not healed, but since they "walk by faith," the symptoms become irrelevant to their faith. For example, if someone were dying of cancer and were suffering with the symptoms, faith would have them say: "I don't care what these symptoms say, the Bible says that I am healed and so I am." Many will think that this is simply denial, the person is refusing to believe that he or she is really sick. In a sense, this is true. When people believe in their heart that they are healed by God, then they can deny the symptoms.

Sin and Lack of Repentance

Sin, by definition, is a turning away from God. And yes, all sin.

for all have sinned and fall short of the glory of God (Rom. 3:23).

Jesus Himself linked sickness with sin.

Afterward Jesus found him in the temple, and said to him, "See, you have been made well. Sin no more, lest a worse thing come upon you" (John 5:14).

It should be noted that this man was still under the Curse of the Law, since Jesus had not yet gone through the atonement. Believers have been redeemed from the Curse of the Law (Gal. 3:13), but sin still destroys people's fellowship with God which is a strong detriment to faith.

So then, if everyone sins and sin undermines faith for healing, how can anyone ever be healed? The same question applies to salvation. How can anyone ever be saved if all are sinners? The answer to both is the faith in Jesus, the redeemer and healer and in His marvelous grace.

Who forgives all your iniquities,
Who heals all your diseases (Ps. 103:3).

And the prayer of faith will save the sick, and the Lord will raise him up. And if he has committed sins, he will be forgiven (James 5:15).

who himself bore our sins in His own body on the tree, that we, having died to sins, might live for righteousness—by whose stripes you were healed (1 Peter 2:24).

If people have any sin for which they have not repented and asked God for His forgiveness, then they should do so now. Then they can ask Him to heal them.

Unforgiveness

The importance of forgiveness in healing was discussed in Chapter Nine. Indeed unforgiveness and the related sins, resentment and hate, can open up people to many diseases such as arthritis and viral infections by lowering one's immunity system. Unforgiveness can be very subtle at times, and it may take some counseling to uncover it. Some people hate another so strongly that they would rather continue to suffer from their illness than to forgive the offending person. Such people should seek an intercessor for deliverance from this destructive emotion. Often when people are delivered from these emotions, they are simultaneously healed.

Envy

Even envy can be a detriment to one's healing.

A sound heart *is* life to the body,
But envy *is* rottenness to the bones (Pr. 14:30).

If people have envy in their lives, they should get rid of it now. They may envy the good health of others, but faith says that they are already healed. If they envy others for something they already have, then the envy is also contrary to faith. Believers are saved Christians, they have nothing to envy over. They should be like Paul:

But indeed I also count all things loss for the excellence
of the knowledge of Christ Jesus my Lord, for whom I

have suffered the loss of all things, and count them as rubbish, that I may gain Christ (Phil. 3:8).

Exhaustion

Physical and mental exhaustion not only brings on disease but also make it very difficult for people to have faith. It is not surprising then that the Lord established the Sabbath as a day of rest (Ex. 31:15). Even medical doctors prescribe rest as a means of combating illness and recovery from trauma.

Jesus has promised to give people rest.

Come to Me, all *you* who labor and are heavy laden, and I will give you rest (Mat. 11:28).

So people can come to Jesus for physical, mental, and spiritual rest.

What about those conditions which cause exhaustion such as depression or sleep disorders? In these cases, as in all illnesses, the sufferer should seek out people with strong faith for healing and have them intercede on their behalf (see Intercessory Prayer, Appendix I).

Summary

The Scriptures show that certain attitudes and actions are contrary to faith and healing. These include the following:

- fear and worry
- doubt and unbelief
- dependence on physical senses
- sin and lack of repentance

- unforgiveness
- envy
- exhaustion.

Harboring any of these will undermine one's faith for healing.

Chapter Twelve
The Tenets of Faith Healing

"...For I am the Lord, the one who heals you."
(Ex. 15:26)

This chapter is a summary of the tenets of faith healing presented in this book. All tenets are totally supported by the Scriptures.

The Scriptures teach that Jesus is the source of all healing and that Satan is the source of all disease. They recognize both the limitations and effectiveness of medical healing and hold it in high esteem. The Scriptures are clear that Jesus is the source of *all* healing, both spiritual and medical. The Scriptures criticize those who seek medical healing without also seeking God. Faith healing and medical healing are allies against sickness, not contrary to one another. When used together they each increase the effectiveness of the other.

Biblical faith is the absolute belief in a promise revealed by God, in spite of no evidence or contrary evidence, to a point where the promise becomes reality in one's heart and mind and appropriate action is taken. Faith for healing is increased by reading and believing God's Word, the Bible. Believers must read the Bible and keep on reading it if they are to develop their faith.

It is absolutely God's will to heal everyone who asks Him in faith. The most fundamental proof that it is God's will to heal is that physical, mental and emotional healing was part of the redemptive act of Jesus being scourged. Jesus not only brought people's sins to the cross but He also brought their

101

sicknesses. The punishment of Jesus' body, as it is commemorated in the Holy Communion bread, is the redeeming act for people's healing. Healing is just as much a part of the atonement as is salvation. The Scriptures talk about salvation and physical healing in the same context. Therefore it is just as much His will to heal people of their diseases as it is His will to forgive them of their sins. God's will to heal is plainly stated as such in the Scriptures. It is also a logical absurdity to assume that it is *not* God's will to heal everyone.

Miracles and healing are just as valid today as they were in the days of the apostles. Jesus Christ is the same yesterday, today, and tomorrow. It is God's will to heal everybody. God is not partial to anyone. God is fully capable of healing any disease and restoring any bodily or mental condition. With God, nothing is impossible. God is willing to heal any and all disease no matter how profound or trivial. Healing does not depend on people's worthiness, only on their faith. God's sovereignty should be viewed as supporting one's faith for healing, not undermining it.

God can and does heal in miraculous and instantaneous ways; however, in many cases it may take some time for the healing to manifest. There are many cases in which people are called upon to not only have faith, but to have patience, diligence, and endurance as well. To have endurance believers must diligently foster their faith. The Scriptures show that one way to foster faith for healing is to develop proper attitudes in one's heart and mind. These include:

- reverence and awe of God
- trust in the Lord
- confidence in the Lord
- righteousness

- forgiveness
- knowledge of God's will
- a merry heart.

These attitudes actually bring about healing.

The Scriptures teach believers to take appropriate action as a natural outgrowth of their faith. Appropriate action for healing includes the following:

- ask the Father in Jesus' name for healing
- believe that He will heal
- speak healing
- thank the Father for healing even before it is manifested
- cast out the spirit of disease in Jesus' name
- read the Word of God, the Bible
- pray for and give care to others
- take Communion discerning the Body of Christ
- seek intercessory faith healing.

People cannot earn their healing. Healing is a gift of God appropriated through faith.

The Scriptures show that certain attitudes, actions, and conditions are contrary to faith and healing. These include the following.

- fear and worry
- doubt and unbelief
- dependence on physical senses
- sin and lack of repentance
- unforgiveness
- envy
- exhaustion.

Harboring any of these will destroy one's faith for healing.

Epilogue

"The sower sows the word.

(Mark 4:14)

When people have heard the healing gospel of our Lord Jesus Christ and have believed it in their hearts, they may have already experienced the healing power of Jesus. However, some may find that they have reached this point with no apparent improvement and are wondering if faith healing is real or not. Satan hates the healing power of Jesus because it thwarts his mission to destroy God's creation, the human body. It is to be expected that he will attack people's faith for healing. Satan will put in their minds many of the misconceptions that have been brought out and exposed in this book.

Most people are familiar with Jesus' parable of the sower.

"Listen! Behold, a sower went out to sow. And it happened, as he sowed, *that* some *seed* fell by the wayside; and the birds of the air came and devoured it. Some fell on stony ground, where it did not have much earth; and immediately it sprang up because it had no depth of earth. But when the sun was up it was scorched, and because it had no root it withered away. And some *seed* fell among thorns; and the thorns grew up and choked it, and it yielded no crop. But other *seed* fell on good ground and yielded a crop that sprang up, increased and produced: some thirty-fold, some sixty, and some a hundred" (Mark 4:3-8).

Later on Jesus interpreted His parable to the twelve disciples. It is instructive to see how this parable applies to people's response to the healing gospel.

It is known from Mark 4:14 that the seed represents the Word of God, the Scriptures.

> "And these are the ones by the wayside where the word is sown. And when they hear, Satan comes immediately and takes away the word that was sown in their hearts" (Mark 4:15).

These people have heard the healing gospel and are filled with doubt and misconceptions. They are unlikely to be healed and therefore further doubt its validity. They are the ones who believe that the healing gospel is nonsense or does not apply today.

> "These likewise are the ones sown on stony ground who, when they hear the word, immediately receive it with gladness; and they have no root in themselves, and so endure only for a time. Afterward, when tribulation or persecution arises for the word's sake, immediately they stumble" (Mark 4:16—17).

These people are likely to have had pangs of joy knowing that God will heal them. They may have already felt the healing power of Jesus, but now the symptoms are back with vengeance. They are filled with doubt and will likely lose whatever healing or faith for healing they may have had. They will talk about all the faith they had, but still were not healed.

> "Now these are the ones sown among thorns; *they are* the ones who hear the word, and the cares of this world,

the deceitfulness of riches, and the desires for other things entering in choke the word, and it becomes unfruitful" (Mark 4:18-19).

These people will simply not have the time to spend reading the Bible or this book because they have higher priorities in their lives. They may pick up either and read a bit, but nothing will really take hold. They may even read this book from cover to cover and mentally agree with everything that is said, but then they will put it down and go on with their lives. These people are too busy with other things and usually forgot completely about the healing promise of God.

"But these are the ones sown on good ground, those who hear the word, accept *it*, and bear fruit: some thirty fold, some sixty, and some a hundred" (Mark 4:20).

Now these people have received the healing gospel with enthusiasm and joy and although their symptoms may have even gotten worse, they cling on to the Word of God knowing that it is truth. They may have even been totally healed while reading the Bible verses in this book. Symptoms or not, they are at peace knowing that God has healed them. They are eager to learn more about faith healing and will go back and read the healing verses again and again until they become familiar and ingrained in their hearts. They read their Bible regularly and will read other books on faith healing. These people are healed and will walk in divine health for the rest of their lives.

May God open the hearts of those who read this book that their faith may bring them healing and divine health.

Appendix I
Methods of Faith Healing

God in His wisdom and grace was given believers different methods of administering and receiving His healing power. Each is from God and they are all equally valid.

Individual Faith

People may appropriate healing for themselves by reading the Word of God concerning healing, believing it, and having faith for it. This is the fundamental purpose behind this book. The Scriptures make it clear that healing is appropriated through individual faith.

> And when He had come into the house, the blind men came to Him. And Jesus said to them, "Do you believe that I am able to do this?" They said to Him, "Yes, Lord." Then He touched their eyes, saying, "According to your faith let it be to you." And their eyes were opened (Mat. 9:28-30).

> And he said to her, "Daughter, your faith has made you well. Go in peace and be healed of your affliction" (Mark 5:34).

> And in Lystra a certain man without strength in his feet was sitting, a cripple from his mother's womb, who had never walked. *This* man heard Paul speaking. Paul, observing him intently and seeing that he had faith to be healed, said with a loud voice, "Stand up straight on your feet!" And he leaped and walked (Acts 14:8-10).

Intercessory Prayer

Intercessory prayer is a prayer prayed by an individual or group for the healing of another individual. The following are examples of intercessory prayer given in the New Testament.

Now when Jesus had entered Capernaum, a centurion came to Him, pleading with Him, saying, "Lord, my servant is lying at home paralyzed, dreadfully tormented."…Then Jesus said to the centurion, "Go your way; and as you have believed, so let it be done for you." And his servant was healed that same hour (Mat. 8:5-6, 13).

Then Jesus answered and said to her, "O woman, great is your faith! Let it be to you as you desire." And her daughter was healed from that very hour (Matt. 15:28).

And behold, one of the rulers of the synagogue came, Jairus by name. And when he saw Him, he fell at His feet and begged Him earnestly, saying, "My little daughter lies at the point of death. Come and lay Your hands on her, that she may be healed, and she will live." So Jesus went with him…Then He took the child by the hand, and said to her, "Talitha, cumi," which is translated, "Little girl, I say to you arise." Immediately the girl arose and walked for she was twelve years *of age* (Mark 5:22-24, 41-42).

So Jesus came again to Cana of Galilee where He had made the water wine. And there was a certain nobleman whose son was sick at Capernaum. When he heard that Jesus had come out of Judea into Galilee, he went to Him and implored Him to come down and heal his son, for he was at the point of death. Then Jesus said to him, "Unless you people see signs and wonders, you will by no means believe." The nobleman said to Him, "Sir, come down before my child dies!" Jesus said to him, "Go your way; your son lives." So the man believed the word that Jesus spoke to him, and he went his way. And as he was now going down, his servants met him and told *him*, saying, "Your son lives" (John 4:46-51)!

Notice that these verses say nothing of the faith of those needing the healing. It was the faith of the centurion, the woman, the synagogue ruler, and the nobleman that Jesus honored.

Many individuals have been healed as the result of church members praying for their healing. It is critically important that the people praying for the healing have strong faith themselves.

Parents can and should pray for the healing of their children. Their faith will bring about healing in their children.

Laying on of Hands

The laying on of hands is another form of intercessory healing in which an individual with strongly developed faith for healing lays his or her hands on the sick person, prays for the healing, and casts the sickness out in the name of Jesus.

they will lay hands on the sick, and they will recover (Mark 16:18).

Now when the sun was setting, all those who had anyone sick with various diseases brought them to Him; and he laid His hands on every one of them and healed them (Luke 4:40).

And it happened that the father of Publius lay sick of a fever and dysentery. Paul went in to him and prayed, and he laid his hands on him and healed him (Acts 28:8).

The effectiveness of this method depends strongly on the faith of the individual who does the laying on of hands. Many miraculous and instantaneous healings have resulted from this method.

Anointing with Oil

This method of faith healing is also intercessory in nature. Here an individual anoints, that is applies, oil to the body of the sick person. Oil has always represented the Holy Spirit, and it is the Holy Spirit who causes the healing to manifest.

And they cast out many demons, and anointed with oil many who were sick, and healed *them* (Mark 6:13).

Is anyone among you sick? Let him call for the elders of the church, and let them pray over him, anointing him with oil in the name of the Lord (James 5:14).

The type of oil used is not at all important. The faith of the individual doing the anointing and that of the person receiving the anointing are most important. Many miraculous and instantaneous healings have resulted from anointing with oil.

Prayer Clothes

Prayer clothes are a less common but very effective means of healing when the sick person can not be brought in for the administration of healing.

Now God worked unusual miracles by the hands of Paul, so that even handkerchiefs or aprons were brought from his body to the sick, and the diseases left them and the evil spirits went out of them (Acts 19:11-12).

In this case a handkerchief or other suitable cloth is prayed over and anointed with the power of the Holy Spirit by an individual with strong faith for healing. The handkerchief is then carried to or sent to the sick person and laid upon him. Such handkerchiefs have literally been sent to the other side of the world with miraculous results.

Speaking Healing

The Lord will heal people by an intercessor simply speaking healing and commanding the sickness to leave in Jesus' name.

Jesus said to him, "Rise, take up your bed and walk." And immediately the man was made well, took up his bed, and walked. And that day was the Sabbath (John 5:8-9).

And in Lystra a certain man without strength in his feet was sitting, a cripple from his mother's womb, who had never walked. This man heard Paul speaking. Paul, observing him intently and seeing that he had faith to be healed, said with a loud voice, "Stand up straight on your feet!" And he leaped and walked (Acts 14:8-10).

Appendix II
Healing Testimonies

For many years the author suffered from severe seasonal allergies, asthma, and eczema. It was necessary to carry several medications with him in case of a sudden attack. Since there were no medical cures for these diseases, the medications were used to simply counter the symptoms. When the author was introduced to the healing Gospel, he put his complete hope and trust in Jesus to heal him and practiced the principles outlined in this book. From that time forward and for the past fifteen years, he has been totally healed of these diseases.

It was this experience that has driven the author to spread the healing Gospel and to enter into the healing ministry. Over the past fifteen years he has been privileged to witness the awesome healing power of the Holy Spirit through his ministry. Hundreds of people have been healed of severe pain, profound orthopedic problems, cancers, diverse viral and bacterial infections, vision and dental problems, allergies, depression and anxiety, high cholesterol, injury, and many others.

To Jesus be all the praise, glory and honor.

The following testimonies are given to show the reality of God's awesome healing power and to build the reader's hope for their personal healing. Only a sample of healings is given here. If the reader's disease or condition is not mentioned, that does not mean that God doesn't heal that type of condition. Indeed God wills, desires, and is infinitely capable of healing any and all diseases and conditions.

Lung Cancer

A middle age man with advanced lung cancer came forward for healing prayer during a church service. During prayer and the laying on of hands this man was totally healed. He testified that a half an hour earlier he had been coughing up blood. He also testified that he had been hit by lightning a short time earlier and that all his injuries from this occurrence were also totally healed by the grace and power of the Holy Spirit.

Cancerous Tumors

An eight-year-old boy was experiencing some problems so he was brought to a doctor for an examination. The doctor ordered a battery of x-rays. The x-rays revealed a series of cancerous tumors on his spine and a large tumor on his brain. His mother stood firmly on the God's promise of healing while his church prayed earnestly for him.

His oncologist ordered an MRI. The young boy was understandably frightened as he was about to be rolled into the MRI machine, so his mother comforted him by assuring him of Jesus' love. When he was rolled out of the MRI he was sound asleep. He later told his mother that he had seen two angels in the machine with him. The MRI showed that the tumors on his spine were totally gone, but the one on his brain was still there. The doctors immediately operated on his head and removed as much of the tumor as they could but had to leave some of it since it was too close to the speech center of his brain. The plan was to use radiation and chemotherapy to destroy the remainder of the tumor.

After the operation, the author went to the hospital to pray for him while he was regaining his strength and before they began the radiation and chemotherapy. Through the laying on of hands in the name of Jesus, the cancer was cursed. What happened next amazed everyone, including the doctors—the tumor remnant began to move around. It eventually moved to a point where the doctors opened him up again and literally plucked it out. All the cancer in his body was gone, and within a few weeks, he was running around like any other eight-year-old boy.

Virulent Lung Infection

A middle aged lady contracted a virulent lung infection and was placed in an intensive care unit in a major hospital. Her condition rapidly worsened and she was put into a drug induced coma. The antibiotics and other medications did not seem to have an effect. The doctors gave her only a 30 percent chance of survival and her relatives were called in to say their "good-byes."

The author visited her three times for prayer and laying on of hands. The first time the Lord stopped the decline in her condition. The second time the Lord began to reverse the condition. The results could actually be seen in the monitoring instruments. The third visit completed the healing.

The doctors told her that she would have diminished lung capacity for the rest of her life because of the scarring on her lungs left by the infection. By the time she left the hospital there was no scarring on her lungs and she has full lung capacity.

Edema

The author was asked to pray for a lady with severe edema of her ankles. The swelling was so severe that it hung over the top of her shoes. By the laying on of hands in the name of Jesus, the swelling immediately shrank and her ankles returned to normal size. It was thrilling to see this awesome move of God. The swelling did not move, it simply disappeared, the excess serous fluid having been obliterated by the power of the Holy Spirit.

Severe Persistent Pain

An eighty-six-year-old lady had been suffering for twelve years with intense, persistent pain in her back and leg. Morphine, which had been useful in the past, was now ineffective. Moreover this poor lady was experiencing muscle spasms which aggravated the pain. Her morale was understandably very low. Through the laying on of hands in the name of Jesus, this lady was totally healed by the power and grace of God.

Vertigo

A lady had been suffering from extreme vertigo for three days caused by a viral infection of the inner ears. By the laying on of hands in the name of Jesus, she was instantly and totally healed. The Lord instantly destroyed the virus and restored the well being of her inner ears.

Arthritis and Short Leg

A lady had severe arthritis in her back and shoulder, lower back pain, and one of her legs was three-quarters of an inch shorter than the other one. All this made her hobble when she walked with a cane, and it gave her trouble getting up from a sitting position. She clearly had the faith to be healed as evidenced by her peace and joy even before her healing was manifested. Through the laying on of hands in the name of Jesus, she was totally healed. Her short leg grew out even with the other by the awesome power of the Holy Spirit.

Digestive Problems

A six-month-old baby boy was born with digestive problems that made him regurgitate any food. The infant had spent most of his life in the hospital being home only for short periods of time. Through the laying on of hands in the name of Jesus, the infant's digestive problems were healed, and he did not have to return to the hospital.

Bursitis

A lady was confined to a wheelchair with crippling bursitis. She was constantly in pain and could not even grip a pen. She was filled with faith to be healed. Through the laying on of hands in the name of Jesus, she was totally healed of the bursitis and could now write with a pen. She also had the little finger on her right hand sticking straight out. She said that as a little girl the doctor had "fixed" her finger, leaving it in its rigid condition. She was now able to bend the finger and make a fist.

Infectious Mononucleosis

A male college student contracted a classic, full-blown case of infectious mononucleosis with swollen glands and a sore and bleeding throat. Through the laying on of hands in the name of Jesus, he was totally healed of the disease in only three days.

High Cholesterol Count

A lady had trouble controlling her blood cholesterol level that had recently been measured at a dangerous count of 400. Through the laying on of hands in the name of Jesus, her next test a few days later was at 208.

www.ingramcontent.com/pod-product-compliance
Lightning Source LLC
LaVergne TN
LVHW051646080426
835511LV00016B/2530